"Mark Plaiss describes in detail the daily routine of a monastic's life. He explains, as well, how the monastic values and routine have influenced his own life, a married layman in the teaching profession. This book might be an invaluable resource for someone discerning a monastic vocation. All the pieces are there."

— Abbot Vincent Bataille
Marmion Abbey
Aurora, Illinois

MONASTIC WISDOM SERIES: NUMBER FIFTY

No End to the Search

Experiencing Monastic Life

Mark Plaiss

α

Cistercian Publications
www.cistercianpublications.org

LITURGICAL PRESS
Collegeville, Minnesota
www.litpress.org

A Cistercian Publications title published by Liturgical Press

Cistercian Publications
Editorial Offices
161 Grosvenor Street
Athens, Ohio 54701
www.cistercianpublications.org

1   2   3   4   5   6   7   8   9

Library of Congress Cataloging-in-Publication Data

Names: Plaiss, Mark, author.
Title: No end to the search : experiencing monastic life / Mark Plaiss.
Description: Collegeville, Minnesota : Cistercian Publications, [2017] |
   Series: Monastic wisdom series ; Number fifty | Includes
   bibliographical references.
Identifiers: LCCN 2017007538 (print) | LCCN 2017034286 (ebook) |
   ISBN 9780879071080 (ebook) | ISBN 9780879071509
Subjects: LCSH: Trappists—Spiritual life. | Cistercians—Spiritual life.
   | Desire—Religious aspects—Christianity. | New Melleray Abbey
   (Peosta, Iowa) | Abbey of Our Lady of Gethsemani (Trappist, Ky.) |
   St. Meinrad Archabbey.
Classification: LCC BX4103 (ebook) | LCC BX4103 .P53 2017 (print) |
   DDC 255/.12—dc23
LC record available at https://lccn.loc.gov/2017007538

For all my students at Carmel Catholic High School,
Mundelein, Illinois

Nor, I think, will a soul cease to seek him even when it has found him. It is not with steps of the feet that God is sought but with the heart's desire; and when the soul happily finds him its desire is not quenched but kindled. Does the consummation of joy bring about the consuming of desire? Rather it is oil poured upon the flames. So it is. Joy will be fulfilled, but there will be no end to desire, and therefore no end to the search.

Saint Bernard of Clairvaux,
Sermon 84 on the Song of Songs

Contents

Abbreviations

CF	Cistercian Fathers series
CS	Cistercian Studies series
CSQ	*Cistercian Studies Quarterly*
MW	Monastic Wisdom series
PG	Patrologia Graeca, ed. J.-P. Migne
RB	Rule of Saint Benedict
S(s)	Sermon(s)

Acknowledgments

I am grateful to the three monastic communities that I discuss in the following pages, and especially to the monks who have welcomed me into their midst. I have received permission from all the monks whom I name; in other cases I have referred to them simply by monastic role. I have also received permission to give the names of friends, family, colleagues, and teachers who appear here. I wish especially to thank Br. Paul Andrew Tanner, OCSO, for his friendship and assistance; Fr. Mark Scott, OCSO, for permission to reproduce the Antiphonary from New Melleray Abbey (appendix A); and Fr. Columba Kelly, OSB, for allowing me to describe him and his chant workshop at St. Meinrad Archabbey and to print the *Graduale Triplex* from the materials he distributed at the workshop (appendix B).

Prelude

The monastery is calling, and you know it.

Thus spoke Bernard:

> This is where the fragrance comes from, this is the goal of
> our running. She had said that we must run, drawn by that
> fragrance, but did not specify our destination. So it is to
> these rooms that we run, drawn by the fragrance that issues
> from them.[1]

But that raises the question, what is the fragrance of the
monastery? Silence, choir, prayer, solitude, community, work?
Each woman, each man, will prefer a different fragrance.
Chanel will woo, but so will Estée Lauder. Just so the fragrance
of the cloister.

You have inhaled that fragrance.

A curious stop in the gift shop at Gethsemani, perhaps. Singing Compline at New Melleray. Maybe a retreat at St. Meinrad
Archabbey. Photographs of Fontenay? The choir of nuns at
Our Lady of the Mississippi, maybe. Perhaps listening to an
account of a friend who was wowed by Saint John's Abbey up
in Collegeville or St. Vincent's in Latrobe.

And now you want more.

Do not dismiss your attraction to the fragrance. The odor
of God is sweet, and the wiles of the Almighty are seductive.
What says the Bride?

---

[1] Bernard of Clairvaux, *On the Song of Songs II*, S 23, trans. Kilian Walsh,
CF 7 (Kalamazoo, MI: Cistercian Publications, 1976), 25.

On my bed at night I sought him
Whom my heart loves—
I sought him, but I did not find him. (Song 3:1)

God is peeking through the lattices for you, and the lattices are in the monastery.

So go there now. Go. Don't just inhale the fragrance; rub your face in it.

Go.

PART ONE

Monasteries

New Melleray Abbey

Dead of night.

A quarter moon wanes in the southeastern sky. My Honda Civic, boasting over 305,000 miles, streaks westbound on Illinois Highway 176. Here are the towns: Marengo, Bellvidere, Rockford, Freeport, Eleroy, Stockton, Woodbine, Elizabeth, Galena, East Dubuque, Illinois; Dubuque, Iowa; and the destination: New Mellery Abbey.

I'll hit Marengo by four in the morning.

Moving from Indiana to Illinois has shaved an hour off the trip to the monastery. Gotta like that.

No radio. No music. No recorded books. No talking heads. Nothing. Just you, God, and the road. All that jazz just distracts, and that's the point: to rid yourself of distractions so you can experience God's mercy, so you can undergo metanoia, so you can attain union with God, so you can evangelize Jesus the Christ.

Your retreat doesn't start at the guesthouse; it begins with the journey to the guesthouse. The journey is a component of the retreat. The journey is important. So don't screw it up driving to the monastery with whatever blaring from your car speakers. Cassian got it right well over a thousand years ago:

> Before the time of prayer we must put ourselves in the state
> of mind we would wish to have in us when we actually pray.
> It is an inexorable fact that the condition of the soul at the
> time of prayer depends upon what shaped it beforehand.[1]

---

[1] Cassian, *Conferences* 10.14, trans. Colm Luibheid, Classics of Western Spirituality (New York: Paulist Press, 1985), 139.

So, you want to pray at the monastery? Create an atmosphere of prayer traveling there.

Hwy 176 ends at Marengo. I hang a left at the light, drive about a half a mile, then, turning right at another light, I pick up US Hwy 20. From that point until the Mississippi River, it's Hwy 20: the Ulysses S. Grant Memorial Highway.

In my rearview mirror? The beginning of daylight.

West of Rockford, Illinois, the terrain changes. More hilly. Up and down, up and down; I feel as if I'm at Cedar Point in Sandusky, Ohio, riding roller coasters. The vistas of Stephenson and Jo Daviess Counties are soothing to see. Cattle graze on steep hills of green grass. Farms nestled in the bottoms. Houses perched on ridges. Hawks glide overhead.

Three hours and twenty minutes after leaving home in Fox Lake, Illinois, I cross the Julien Dubuque Bridge and glide into Dubuque, Iowa. At the stoplight at the foot of the bridge I hang a left and head south.

I follow US 151 as it splits off of US 61 just south of Dubuque and drive about five miles. Hang a right onto Monastery Road.

A few minutes later a building swings into view as I roll down a hill that fades right. I can make out the roofline of the monastery. When I reach the bottom of that hill the whole southern face of the stone quadrangle swings into view. I slow the car and turn right onto the long circular driveway.

I park in front of the guesthouse. I pop the trunk, remove my gear, and walk to the doors of the place. A canvas bag is slung over my left shoulder. I drag a red suitcase behind me.

I haul all my stuff to the third-floor landing, where I encounter a door bearing this sign:

Monastic Enclosure
Associates only

I pull on the door and pass through. One of the four rooms in the Monastic Center is occupied, room 303. I move on to room 305. Both of those rooms look out over the garth, while the other two rooms opposite them look out over the parking lot. You want one of the rooms looking out over the garth; the rooms looking out over the parking lot are too noisy.

I drop my gear in the room, step to the window, and yank on the cord, raising the blinds. The late May sun splashes through. I crank open the windows, and the mild morning air rushes in.

Feels good.

From the closet I remove a hooded gray smock; I slip it over my head. It falls to my upper thighs. I sit on the bed and remove my Reeboks and slip on my "choir shoes," a pair of slip-on sneakers. I snatch the key on the desk and leave the room.

Back down the stairs I go. At the bottom of the stairwell is a locked door. I unlock the door and step through. Now I'm in the cloister. I can smell the aroma of cooked food. Hanging on the cloister wall to my left is an icon of Madonna and Child. I ask for her intercession. I step over to the window that looks out onto the garth. Now that I am on ground level I can see beads of dew clinging to the grass.

The door I had walked through clicks gently shut behind me. I step over to another door that leads from the cloister and into the abbey chapel. I pull it open and step through.

Light pours through the arched windows high above me. I glance to my left; no one is in the guest area. Course, why should there be? Terce doesn't begin for another hour.

I turn right, east, and walk past the organ. Midway up the choir stalls I halt and make a deep bow toward the altar. I step into the north choir and slip into the first choir stall to the east of the break. I kneel down on the tile floor and thank God for bringing me to New Melleray Abbey in safety. I pray that this retreat will bring me to conversion.

It'll take the remainder of the day and then some to settle down. The rhythm of the house takes its time to envelop you; you can't rush it. Before me are five days of prayer, working in the garden, and conversion.

It is good to be back in my monastic home.

Let me describe my room to you, room 305 in the Monastic Center. High-school marble floor. A desk, a twin bed, a cushioned chair, a wastepaper can, a closet in which hang three hooded smocks as well as a tangle of black wire hangers. Walking from this main section, you move to the bathroom. First is the sink with a medicine cabinet. Next a shower. Finally the toilet. Two windows are in the bathroom; two windows are in the main room. Blinds are in all four windows.

On the bed are a fresh bath towel, hand towel, and washcloth, folded up nicely. A plastic cup sealed in plastic rests smartly atop the towels. The key to the cloister is on the desk. That's exactly what you're supposed to see when you first enter your room. You see, when you vacate the room at the end of your retreat, you are supposed to clean the room yourself. That entails sweeping the floor, dusting off the desk, cleaning the shower, toilet, and sink, changing the sheets on the bed, and replacing the pillowcases. More often than not you discover that is actually the case when you first enter the room. Men, though, tend to be slovenly creatures, and some don't always comply with the cleaning instructions. There have been times when I've had to do extensive cleaning before occupying my room, but those times have been few.

There are four rooms within the Monastic Center. At the northeast corner of the hall within the Center is a kitchen replete with fridge, sink, microwave, and a table on which sits a toaster. I've never seen people sitting at the table. At the southwest corner of the hall is a little library that has some good titles. A desk with a telephone is in there too.

It's quiet.

Real convenient are the washer and dryer in the room that is just outside the south end of the Monastic Center. Go out the door, and boom, there it is on your left.

I say *convenient*, because your clothes will get real dirty when you are a Monastic Center guy, and so the washer and dryer so close at hand is a blessing. Why do your clothes get so dirty when you are a Monastic Center guy?

I've got three words for you: Brother Placid, garden.

Now, I don't live with Br. Placid. Living with a person and visiting a person once a year for five days are two different things. So my picture of Br. Placid is going to be somewhat different, I'm presuming, from the picture the monks who live with him have.

I love the guy. Br. Placid is the keeper of the monastery garden. He knows all things agricultural. The man is eighty-eight years old. He grew up on a farm in Minnesota. He fought in the Korean War and entered the monastery soon thereafter as a brother. His head is bald, his eyes are Windex-blue, and his skin is tanned. He's not tall, but that's also misleading, because he stands and walks in a stoop because of a back and neck malady, most likely the result of decades of clawing and scratching vegetables from the fertile Iowa dirt. He can wrestle a tiller onto the rear end of a tractor single-handedly. He has a nice grin.

When you are a Monastic Center guy, your afternoon work assignment is with him.

Now if you hail from the metropolis, as I do, your initial work with Br. Placid is bewildering. He tells you to do things that you are clueless how to perform. However, if you return to the Monastic Center year after year, as I have done, you slowly catch on to what he wants. The key is patience, with both him and yourself. He is not gruff, but you quickly grasp that there is only one way to do things: Placid's way. Believe me, you'll learn things you never thought you would learn.

Such as attaching a tiller to a tractor; planting corn, melons, pumpkins, and trees; erecting a hothouse; stringing a fence; placing a floor in a grain silo; digging up potatoes, radishes, and garlic; trimming apple trees; picking apples; the *proper* method of hoeing weeds; mending a beehive; picking corn (sounds simple enough; Placid's method has nuance); driving fence posts into a nearly frozen ground with a fifty-pound "pounder"; removing boulders from the ground; closing down all the water outlets in the garden for the winter; sticking field-marking flags in the ground at designated intervals (intervals determined by a trusty pole of approximately 4.5 feet). After he gets to know you, he'll have you drive his fifty-year-old Ford pickup truck around the grounds, as in, "Ok, take the truck over yonder and pick up those radishes you picked earlier."

My all-time-favorite Placid job involved peanut butter.

One day Placid hands my friend and fellow Monastic Center confrere Hal Jopp a bowl of peanut butter. Then turning to me Placid says, "Dip this goo [the peanut butter] into those cups you see every so many feet. I'll go over the way and turn off the juice. When you see me wave my hat, you can go."

What?

Placid had a single-wire electric fence around a large section of the garden. Well, deer and other critters were still getting into the garden, so Placid attaches these cups to the wire. The cups were about the size of a half-dollar in circumference, and about a half-inch deep. Hal and I were supposed to walk the circumference of this section of the garden. Hal would hold the bowl of goo, and when we approached the section of wire that had the cup, I would dip my fingers into the bowl of goo and drop the goo from my fingers into the cup. Before doing that, however, Placid had to turn off the electric current (however, Placid did offer *not* to turn off the current—I declined the offer).

Now, the electric wire was running through the cup, the idea being that the peanut butter would attract the deer, and when the deer dipped its tongue into the cup to eat the peanut butter, ZAP! The shock would not be so strong as to harm the animal, but strong enough to discourage further entry into Placid's garden. Far as I know it was successful.

The things you learn at a monastery.

Terce, at 9:15 a.m., will be my first office of the day, of my retreat. I like the Little Hours. Sunlight floods through the windows, and upon entering the chapel, the chapel seems to be saying, "Come in and pray!" The long night of intense prayer and *lectio* is over. The daily Mass celebrated. We now roll into a more relaxed mode of prayer. The three psalms at each of the Little Hours are short, familiar, and fun to sing.

Using my key I walk through the locked door. I'm now standing in the southwest corner of the cloister. I step over to a window that looks onto the garth. I like to wait there until the first bell rings for the office. I see birds flit this way and that in the garth.

The monastery bell ringer rings the first bell for Terce, and with that I enter the chapel through the southwest door. I walk east, hugging the north choir stalls, and when I reach the break in the stalls, I bow. Then I slip into the north choir, stopping at the first stall east of the break. I kneel down on the tile floor, slipping my feet into the stall. I thank God for allowing me to worship him at this hour of Terce, and I pray that I will make this time of prayer fruitful.

I climb back to my feet and check out the two books on the stand in front of me: the antiphonary and the psalter. The antiphonary is a three-ring notebook divided by week, day, and hour. It provides the antiphon we will sing and informs us of the specific psalms we will chant. Up for today are Psalms 119, 120, and 121 (Greek numeration). The antiphon appears to be simple. In regard to the psalms, the community will go through the entire psalter every two weeks. The psalms are divided into two one-week cycles designated as Odd-numbered Weeks and Even-numbered Weeks. Since I am at New Melleray during the Ninth Week in Ordinary Time, the community is in Odd-numbered Weeks.

Monks begin to file in. They are not wearing the cowl or cloak as they had done at Vigils and Lauds. Most of them enter the chapel through the southeast door. On doing so they dip their fingers into the holy water font, bless themselves, and, turning toward the altar, bow. On arriving at their place in choir, and after a moment in knelt prayer, the monks stand, check out the books on the stand, then either sit in the stall or turn and face east, awaiting the second bell, which signals the beginning of the Hour. I see no novices, no postulants in choir. Br. Charles, temporary professed, is in the south choir. He is the one who sometimes turns on the overhead lights in the chapel.

I like being in the north choir, because I'm right up against windows, and since I'm here in late May and early June, those windows are open. The grass has been recently mowed, and you just can't beat the smell of freshly mowed grass when you're at prayer.

The stalls in the south choir are full down to the break. Over in the north choir, it's the same, though Fr. Xavier fills the first stall to the west of the break.

The second bell rings and we blast off. Those who had been sitting now rise and face east. Brother Organist strikes the tone on the organ down at the southwest end of the choir. A lone monk rides on that tone, singing, *O God, come to my assistance.* The remainder of us then chime in, *O Lord, make haste to help.* Then, turning to face the space between the two choirs, the monks bow and sing the doxology:

> Glory be to the Father and to the Son
> And to the Holy Spirit.
> As it was in the beginning, is now and ever shall be
> World without end, Amen.

If there is a space between monks, that is, if a monk is not present in his stall, then now the monks move up from west to east to fill in those empty spaces. Trappists like to pray all cozy-like! (Or as my mother would say, "togetherness.") Having done that, we sing the hymn.

Since this is a ferial day, and since we are in Ordinary Time, the hymn is as follows:

> Come Holy Spirit ever One, with God the Father and the
> Son.

It is the hour, our souls possess with your full flood of
holiness.
Let flesh and heart and lips and mind sound forth our
witness to mankind
and love light up our mortal flame, till others catch the living
flame.
Almighty Father, hear our cry, through Jesus Christ our Lord
most high
and with the Spirit Paraclete, whose reign the endless ages
greet. Amen.

Brother Organist quickly gives the tone on the organ for the
antiphon. This will be the only antiphon for the three psalms.
The cantor begins, and then we all join in to finish. As I said,
the antiphon at the Little Hours, especially on a ferial day, is
short and simple and to the point. I like that. Antiphons can
be quite complicated on feasts and solemnities. It takes a voice
like the subprior's to carry those. Today's antiphon at Terce,
however, I can handle.

After the antiphon we blast off with the psalms.

The chant we're using today for the psalms I like very much.
Again, very simple. And since the tone for each of the three
psalms is the same, one psalm melds right into the other in a
seamless whole. Sometimes I hate when we stop chanting the
psalms, because I'm in a groove or on a roll, and I just want to
keep going!

With the conclusion of the psalms, we once again turn and
face east. The reader gives us a brief reading from the Bible. A
Marian versicle is then pitched. At Terce at this time of the year
it is this:

In the bush seen by Moses, as burning yet unconsumed,
We recognize the preservation of your glorious virginity.
O Mother of God, intercede for us.

The abbot gives the dismissal, and the Hour is prayed. Ten
minutes tops. What does Benedict instruct? "In community,
prayer should always be brief" (RB 20.5).

My neighbor in choir to the west of me is frequently Fr. Xavier. This would be a good time to mention another monk who was frequently my neighbor in choir over the years, just to the west of me.

Br. Felix.

I first met the man in 1997. He was the guest master. I was struck initially by his quick, wide grin and his ears; they seemed to stick out a little. On my first visit to the Monastic Center, Br. Felix showed me the ropes.

"Are you familiar with the choir and the books?" he asked me.

"No."

"You have your key?"

I held it up for him to see.

So we walked from the office there in the guesthouse to the door at the southwest entrance to the cloister. We entered the chapel, and he showed me my place in the north choir, where the Monastic Center guys take their place. He pointed out the books on the stand and the ordo. He gave me a basic lesson in how to use them. But it was the singing in choir that he most emphasized.

"Don't sing too loud. Blend in with the monks. At the end of the phrase, don't sing as loud, soften your voice."

After that, Br. Felix walked me around the cloister showing me the refectory and other rooms just off the cloister.

Over the years I sometimes worked with Br. Felix in the old workshop, not the new plant across the road where Trappist Caskets is now located, but in the older building. I would help him sand down the wood used for the caskets.

One Saturday afternoon we finished work there, and he and I walked back to the house together. It was a gorgeous late October day, not a cloud in the big blue Iowa sky. The air was crisp and smelled like autumn. The leaves on the trees had peaked in color. We were both tired, but Br. Felix wore that big grin of his.

"No work tomorrow!" he said. "Much prayer!"

He was so delighted with his life, with that day, with that moment.

But mostly I saw Br. Felix in choir. When I made my first entrance in choir at any given retreat, Br. Felix flashed that smile and gave me a slight wave. Sometimes, he would shake my hand.

I liked hearing him read. His voice was strong but never jarring, and he knew how to give a line just the right amount of emphasis.

At this retreat, though, he is no longer my neighbor in choir. He died on Saturday, April 23, 2016, a little over a month before I arrived. I would very much have liked to attend his funeral, but since school was still in session, I could not make it. I was told the turnout for his funeral was large.

Br. Felix entered New Melleray in 1950. He was eighty-seven years old when he died.

Do you like to eat? Is good food something you look forward to? Well, then, the guesthouse at New Melleray Abbey is your kind of place.

Really, the food is excellent. The monks may be vegetarians, but you needn't be. Chicken, roast beef, and the best meat loaf I've ever tasted, period. Wicked mashed potatoes. Always a salad. Vegetables fresh from Br. Placid's garden. I've seen radishes that I know we had picked just the day before. Hearty soups. Great desserts. Yum, yum!

The main meal of the day is the noon meal, served right after Sext. The Monastic Center guys eat together in a little room just off the main dining room. It is there that Br. Placid stops by during breakfast to tell you what you're going to be doing during afternoon work.

However, some Monastic Center guys don't eat there. Take Silent Stan, for example. Silent Stan was in the Monastic Center one time, and not only did he not take a single meal with the remainder of the guys, but he never spoke a word to anybody. He came down to the dining room, filled his tray, and then went back to his room to eat. During afternoon work, he did not engage in conversation. I only heard his voice in choir, but not at Mass. For some reason, he retreated to the guest area of the chapel for Mass.

I could never determine if he was naturally taciturn or if he was scrupulously following the ninth step of humility as prescribed in the Rule: "a monk controls his tongue and remains silent" (RB 7.56). But he was not a monk. Perhaps he was practicing to be one.

Be that as it may, let's get back to the food. As I said, the main meal of the day is at noon, and it's always top-notch. Breakfast is a simple affair: boiled eggs, cheese, cereal (I go for the Raisin Bran), and something along the lines of banana bread. There's a toaster. Orange juice and coffee.

The evening meal is often leftovers from the noon meal, or cold cuts of ham or turkey might be offered. For the evening meal, though, on Sundays no meal is offered. So what is a Monastic Center guy to do? Drive off in a snit to nearby Dubuque and delight in McDonalds' fare?

Of course not! All you do is go down to the kitchen, find the walk-in refrigerators, and help yourself to whatever is there. And there's always something good. Dig out a plate, slap the food on the plate, shove it in the microwave, and voilà! Dinner is served! However, since Monastic Center guys don't often spend Sunday nights there, I have frequently eaten the Sunday evening meal all alone.

Silent Stan would love it.

Usually when I'm in choir I wear a pair of khaki pants and either a pair of sandals (sockless) or some canvas shoes that won't squeak when I walk on the tile floor in the chapel or the marble floor in the cloister.

But not at None, which cranks up at one forty-five. At that Hour I'm clad in jeans and shod in boots, because right after the Hour I have to meet Br. Placid out front at two o'clock. To save time I wear my work clothes into choir, as opposed to changing clothes right after None and *then* going down to meet Br. Placid.

A few minutes after two o'clock, here he comes in that old Ford pickup truck. It's a 1966 special. Honest. To say it has seen better days is an understatement. It's running, but barely. When I slip into the cab, we chug away. *Chug* being the key-word there.

"Think they'd buy you a new truck?" I ask him.

He just laughs.

Placid is dressed in his usual work attire: blue bib overalls over a tattered shirt, his brown scapular of Mount Carmel clearly visible beneath his shirt. The scapular is nearly jabbing him in the neck. He's wearing heavy brown boots.

I gently slap his shoulder with my leather work gloves I'm holding in my right hand.

"What's on the agenda for today?" I ask.

"Well, I thought we'd plant some melons and then some corn."

The truck lumbers around the corner of the monastery, and we jostle over the freshly mowed grass toward "the pump house." Actually it's a toolshed, but behind the shed is a water faucet.

Placid stops the truck in front of the shed. As we climb out of the truck he says, "You'll need a hoe and trowel." So he disappears into the darkened shed and soon emerges with said tools. He places them in the bed of the truck.

"How about some nice cool water before we start?" he asks. We step behind the shed, and he says, "You go first. Get that water cold for me!" I twist the handle and gulp down some water, and he follows.

"Well, let's pray over there," and he points to the shade of a nearby tree. The day is brilliantly sunny, not a cloud to be found in the big blue Iowa sky. The temperature is probably around eighty, and the humidity is not too bad.

We sit down on the concrete ledge of an enclosed bed of lettuce. Placid removes his hat, places his hands on his knees, bows his head and begins, "Hail Mary, full of grace, the Lord is with thee." I chime in at the "Holy Mary, Mother of God." We pray three Hail Marys.

Then Placid invokes a litany of two saints, Saint Joseph and Saint Maria Goretti, and I reply, "Pray for us!"

And with that we're ready to head out for work.

We start back to the truck, but Placid says, "Oh, forgot the seeds." So he steps back into the shed and fetches the seeds, which are in little plastic bags. "Stick these in your pockets," he says to me.

We get back in the truck, and we lumber over the field to a large tilled garden. We walk about twenty yards into the garden, in which there are little field flags. "This is where I left off this morning." Placid then instructs me on how to plant melon seeds. Kneeling down in the dirt at one of the field flags he says, "Make a hole like this," and he inserts his index finger in the ground. "Then drop three seeds from your bag there into the hole." He drops three seeds taken from his bag. "Then knuckle it," and he demonstrates. With the knuckles of three fingers he pushes down gently over the hole where he planted the seeds.

"Ok?" he asks me.

"Got it. Hole with finger, three seeds, knuckle it, at each flag."

He then walks to the other end of the garden. We would meet in the middle.

For nearly the next hour Placid and I plant melon seeds. I kneel down on one knee when I plant, but I notice Placid simply bends over. My barking back tells me not to emulate Placid. I accidently spill my bag of seeds at one point, but I manage to retrieve them all and replace them in the plastic bag.

When we finish with the melons we hop back into the truck and jostle over the fields to a much larger tilled garden. Here we are to plant corn. Again the little field flags dot the dirt. However, in this field four people are already planting. Not monks, but a woman and her three children, two of whom are teens.

"Take your trowel," Placid tells me as we get out of the truck. I reach into the bed of the truck and snatch it up. Meanwhile, Placid steps over to where the other four are already planting. I follow, and Placid introduces me to them.

After Placid is sure the planting is going properly, he and I walk through the dirt to the other end of the garden. I would say this garden is nearly one hundred yards long and about a quarter of the width of a football field.

Unlike with the melons, Placid and I work together planting the corn.

"Got your seeds?" he asks me as we approach the first flag marking where we'll plant. I show him the clear bag of orange-red seeds. "Give me the trowel," he says. I do.

"I'll dig the hole," he says, "and you'll drop in six seeds from that bag." And that's what we do for the next hour. At first I am scrupulous about making sure I remove exactly six seeds from the bag. But since that takes too much time, I begin simply pouring into my hand an approximate amount. Since Placid doesn't object, I figure he is good with that. We talk some, but not much. I come within an ace of asking Placid about the Korean War, but decide against it. If you really want to get him going, bring up that Police Action. We manage to plant the entire garden, but only because of the other four.

At about ten after four Placid announces that it is quitting time. We walk back to the truck and drive to the shed. I clean the trowel, and we both get a drink of water.

"Can you make it back home yourself?" Placid asks me. "I want to go back to them," meaning the four who helped planting.

"Sure," I say. So I walk back to the monastery, and Placid rumbles away in his truck back to the garden.

The first thing I have to do on arriving back at the house is remove my shoes before stepping in. My shoes are caked with dirt.

The climb up to the third floor, where the Monastic Center is housed, seems tougher now than when I first arrived. I shower, and then I haul my dirty clothes over to the washer down the hall. On returning to my room I just sit with a cup of water and stare out the window. The shadows are long out in the garth, and the birds jabber away. The fan near my bed hums.

The work was good today.

Yet no one comes to a monastery to work in a garden. No one says to himself or herself, "You know, I think I'll go to a monastery so I can work in a garden."

When a man or woman enters a monastery, he or she is asked, "Why are you here? What do you seek?"

What's the answer?

I open one eye as I lie in bed. The red glow of the alarm clock reads 2:57 a.m. Perfect. I reach over and turn off the alarm I had set for three o'clock the night before.

I roll out of bed. I step to the windows and drop the blinds. I had them open while I was sleeping to allow the air to circulate better. I go into the bathroom and drop the blinds there as well. Now I flip on the lights.

Stepping to the sink I splash some water on my face in order to wipe seven hours of sleep out of my eyes. I brush my teeth and gargle. My mind somewhat clearer now, I quickly dress. I make up the bed. Before leaving the room I slip the gray hooded smock over my head. I snatch the key to the cloister.

I leave my room and descend three floors' worth of stairs. Reaching the door to the cloister I insert the key, open the door, and step into the southwest corner of the cloister. All is quiet in these wee small hours of the morning, and I am self-conscious about the noise when the door clicks shut behind me. The cloister is dimly lit, nightlight capacity illumination. At the far end of the western range, I can barely discern a ghostly figure approaching me. The figure is clothed in a white cowl with the hood up. The long sleeves of the cowl nearly drag the floor.

I slip into the church through the southwest door. Except for the sanctuary candle at the far eastern end of the chapel there is no light at all in the chapel. I take that back; there is the spotlight in the guest area.

I reach the stalls in the north choir, and, letting the fingers of my left hand gently glide over the top of the stalls, I walk until my fingers tell me I'm at the break in the choir (it's difficult for me to *see* the break). I bow. I then step into the choir and take my place in the first stall to the east of the break.

I kneel on the tile floor and thank God for allowing me to pray at this time of Vigils.

I rise quietly as possible, not wanting to disturb Fr. Tom, who is always in choir when I arrive for Vigils. I lower the wooden seat and sit. I take a few deep breaths. Stars flicker through the windows above the south choir. I've been in choir before, at Vigils, when moonlight streams through those windows and splashes down on the floor between the north and south choirs. Loved that!

So quiet. "Lord Jesus Christ, Son of God, have mercy on me, a sinner." With my eyes shut and my chin slightly lowered, I repeat the Jesus Prayer several times until finally I let it fade away, and I just sit there and allow God to overshadow me.

Here comes Br. Placid. I can tell by his stoop. He does not wear the cowl, but the cape. Far as I know, he's the only solemnly professed monk to wear the cape instead of the cowl. At any rate, he shuffles through the southwest door of the chapel and approaches the north choir. Before slipping into the choir he stops and makes a profound bow. He holds the bow for a few moments before stepping to the choir and taking a seat in the far western portion of the choir. He coughs. He blows his nose.

More monks enter the chapel and take their places in choir. Presently, a monk comes walking down the length of the north choir, walking east. I notice he does not need to glide his hand over the tops of the stalls. He steps expertly through the break and by me, his cowl swishing, and slips into a stall several down from where I sit.

Someone other than Placid, someone down at the far eastern end of the north choir, coughs and blows his nose. This seems to open a floodgate of throat clearing and coughing, the sound of which bounces off the stone walls of the chapel.

A few minutes pass, and then I hear it: the chimes from within the house. It's not a bell ringing. Imagine someone striking several bars on a xylophone in quick succession. Sounds like that. It seems to be saying: it's time to wake up, boys, and pray. It's three fifteen in the morning.

Minutes pass, and more and more monks enter the chapel, most of them from the northeast door. They dip their fingers into the holy water as they pass through the door (wish there were such a stoup at the southwest door) and bow before the altar, then take their place in choir.

Some lights snap on. Now a sea of white robes rises. I, too, stand. We begin organizing the two books before us: the antiphonary and the psalter. However, some kind soul has already placed those books that are in front of me at their proper spot for the day and Hour. Great!

Most of the monks now turn, stand, and face east, though a few remain seated. Most of the overhead lights are extinguished except for the spotlight over the ambo. They are waiting for the bell.

The monastery bell ringer rings them at three thirty.

A monk approaches the ambo. He takes a moment, then begins reciting Psalm 133:

> *O come, bless the Lord,*
> *all you who serve the Lord,*
> *who stand in the house of the Lord,*
> *in the courts of the house of our God.*

Then all say, *O Lord, open my lips, and my mouth shall declare your praise.*

The monk at the ambo finishes the psalm:

> *Lift up your hands to the holy place*
> *and bless the Lord through the night.*
> *May the Lord bless you from Zion,*
> *He who made both heaven and earth.*

All repeat, *O Lord, open my lips, and my mouth shall declare your praise.*

The monk at the ambo says, *Pray at all times in the Spirit, with all prayer and supplication. To that end, keep alert with all perseverance.*

And the brothers conclude with the final petition: *O Lord, open my lips, and my mouth shall declare your praise.*

With that, Vigils has begun.

Vigils is divided into two nocturns, each one including a rather long reading and three psalms (or one long psalm, such as Psalm 88). The readings are from Scripture or the Fathers. A long pause, with lights out, separates the two nocturns.

With regard to Vigils, the Constitution for the Order of Cistercians of the Strict Observance reads:

> In the sober anticipation of the coming of Christ, following the tradition of the Order, the hours before sunrise are appropriately consecrated to God by the celebration of Vigils, by prayer and meditation.

Then the punch line:

> The brothers' hour of rising is so determined that Vigils maintains its nocturnal character.[2]

The OCSO was shrewd to maintain that "nocturnal character." For Vigils is *the* hour of prayer for monks. The night is quiet and so conducive to deep prolonged prayer. Terrence Kardong puts it this way: "It can be said that Vigils is the Office most characteristic of monks, while Matins and Vespers are the property of the whole Church."[3] New Melleray begins Vigils at three thirty, Gethsemani at three fifteen, and the Abbey

[2] www.ocso.org/wp-content/uploads/2016/05/X-EN-Constitutions-of-the-Monks-2014.pdf, C.23.

[3] Terrence Kardong, *Benedict's Rule: A Translation and Commentary* (Collegeville, MN: Liturgical Press, 1996), 169.

of Genesee at two twenty-five. (Really? Couldn't make it two thirty?)

Yet Vigils also has the potential to be utter drudgery. André Louf, who was a Trappist monk and abbot, put it this way:

> The calm of the night does not long remain a peaceful invitation to prayer. It becomes oppressive, inviting the novice to a thousand ways to escape. All the activities of the day start to occupy his mind before their time with a demanding urgency. And there seems much to be said in favor of a return to his own room for a further short sleep. Surely, he will be better able to meet the coming day after some extra rest? These suggestions do not come to him as idle insinuating thoughts, but with strength which will overpower him if he hesitates at all. In this way he discovers the ambivalence of his heart. He cannot see any sign of determination and will which were so evident earlier. He discovers how little the night vigils attract him, though he formerly saw them as the most beautiful elements of the monk's life. Now they are only a nuisance.[4]

At home I probably rise at three o'clock to pray Vigils about once a week. My point: it's easy enough to rise for Vigils at the monastery when you know you're only going to be there for five days. For a lifetime?

With the conclusion of Vigils I remain seated in my stall. I like to pray Centering Prayer there. Five minutes after the conclusion of Vigils all the monks have left the chapel except Fr. David. Sometimes others remain for meditation, but I usually see only Fr. David, a few stalls to the east of me, when I finish Centering and leave the chapel.

I return to room 305 usually between four fifteen and four thirty, depending on the day (if the day is a solemnity, the time for Vigils is extended). I then fix myself some hot chocolate

---

[4] André Louf, *The Cistercian Way*, CS 76 (Kalamazoo, MI: Cistercian Publications, 1983), 51–52.

(Land O'Lakes Mint & Chocolate) down in the kitchen at the west end of the Monastic Center. I bring the hot cup back to my room and begin a long session of *lectio*, usually about forty-five minutes. When I first started going to the Monastic Center I would remain clad in my hooded smock and pray *lectio* with the hood of the smock up over my head, *just like the monks do*! I no longer do that. It smacks too much of pretending, thus making it inauthentic and unreal. Today, I just pull off the smock when I return to my room. (I also don't wear the smock during meals down in the dining room—because I don't want to spill food on the smock while eating. I can be such a slob!)

Scripture. Silence. Stars outside my window, then the creeping dawn. Birds awake. Peaceful. The ongoing struggle for conversion, denial of self, and union with God.

Why are you here? What do you seek?

Precisely that.

> Have I made a find! I was surfing the Internet and came across the web page for a monastery called New Melleray Abbey. I was exploring it when I came across a program offered at the monastery called the Associate Program in something called the Monastic Center. This program is for laymen who want a deeper commitment to the contemplative life than simply a few days of retreat each year. In this program the Associate lives in the Monastic Center and prays with the monks in choir. The stay in the Monastic Center can be longer than the usual several days. BINGO! THIS IS WHAT I'VE BEEN SEEKING! I'm so excited about this I could bust!

So I wrote in my journal on Wednesday, April 2, 1997, upon discovering New Melleray and the Monastic Center. I had to get there! Now it just so happened that my older son, then fourteen years old, had recently received the sacrament of confirmation. As part of his confirmation gift, he and I had already decided to make an overnight retreat at a monastery. Our initial choice had been Gethsemani, but on my calling down there I was told that Gethsemani didn't allow (at least then) children my son's age to make a retreat there. That's why I was surfing the internet that day when I happened upon New Melleray; I was trying to find a monastery that would accept a fourteen-year-old.

By April 9 I had reserved our retreat at New Melleray for late July. At that retreat I would make my application to the Monastic Center.

My son and I arrived at New Melleray for our retreat on the morning of July 30, 1997. We were given room 316 in the guesthouse. After None that day I walked down to the guesthouse office. Fr. Bernard was at the desk. I asked him about the Monastic Center. He said Br. Gilbert was in charge of that; however, Br. Gilbert was not in the house at the moment but was in Dubuque for a doctor's appointment. Fr. Bernard took my name and room number and told me Br. Gilbert would get in touch with me later.

About five o'clock that afternoon a knock came at our door. It was Br. Gilbert. I invited him in, but he asked if we could just step into an empty conference room next door. We did so. He took down some basic information from me: name, age, home address, parish I attended, etc. I told him of my interest in the Monastic Center. I explained my having begun to pray the Liturgy of the Hours the year before. I told him the Monastic Center appeared to be a place where I could delve deeper into God.

He said there was absolutely no problem with my becoming an Associate. He said that the Monastic Center was booked up for the remainder of the summer, but September and October were clear for me to come back. He had forgotten to bring with him an official application form but said that after Vespers he would stop by and give me one. He did so. I filled it out and gave it to him.

My family and I were living in La Porte, Indiana, at this time, and when I told Br. Gilbert where that town was located, he said that there was a priest from Kalamazoo, Michigan—about a hundred miles northeast of La Porte—who came to the Monastic Center. So I wasn't the only one who lived hours away from the Monastic Center but wanted to be there!

Our meeting was short; Vespers was approaching at five thirty. Br. Gilbert was not in habit, having come directly to my room from his appointment in Dubuque. He thanked me for my interest in the Monastic Center and wished me and my son well on our current retreat. When my son and I left our room to go to Vespers, we walked down the third-floor hall to reach the stairwell. At the end of the hall, there at the top of the stairs was the door to the Monastic Center. A sign was on the door. It said:

> *Monastic Enclosure*
> *Associates only*

Soon I would be an Associate and able to walk through that door.

I returned on Monday, September 22, 1997. I was housed in room 300. I was very excited. Sext would be the first Hour down in the choir. I wrote the following in my journal afterward:

> By the grace of God through the life, passion, death, and resurrection of Jesus of Nazareth, and with the intercession of the Blessed Mother of God, I appeared for the first time in monk's choir, chanting Sext on this Monday the 22nd day of September 1997, the 25th week in Ordinary Time.

Later that day, my first afternoon of work with Br. Placid, I helped put down a floor in a grain silo, followed by washing potatoes and tomatoes.

I was on my way.

One of my neighbors in the Monastic Center that year was "St. Louis" Paul Tanner (he hailed from The Gateway to the West). He was discerning his vocation to the Trappists and to New Melleray. Obviously he discerned well. Br. Paul Andrew, OCSO, is now a solemnly professed monk at New Melleray, the vocations director, head of the Monastic Center, and the book review editor of *Cistercian Studies Quarterly* (among other things; I'm sure he has other duties within the house). And I can say I knew him when!

Paul was not the only man in the Monastic Center that year discerning a monastic vocation. There were two others. As to their whereabouts and stations in life now, I am clueless.

You see, the Monastic Center is basically a space for men discerning a monastic vocation, specifically to New Melleray. The space is an introduction to solitude and communal prayer. In a sense the Monastic Center is the first hint (and I emphasize *hint*) of monastic life. Can you handle solitude? Can you pray with other people in a prescribed fashion? Can you dive into *lectio* on a consistent basis? Can you handle not speaking to others from the conclusion of Compline until after Mass the next day? The Monastic Center clearly occupies a space between the general retreat house and the dwelling of the monks living there. No fee is charged, nor is there a time limit on how long one may stay. Men who aspire to join the community, such as Paul Tanner back in 1997, often spend a month or so here. That married men, such as me, are allowed in this space at all is a wonder to me.

A married man with children in a monastery. But it gets even stranger. I grew up a by-God Baptist.

Here was a typical Sunday morning in the summer when I was young. My dad, his brother, and I would drive to a lake in a state forestry to fish for bluegill and bass. On the thirty-minute drive to the lake Dad would tune the radio to some station from deep in Kentucky. This station broadcast a preacher who yelled and screamed and pounded on the podium so much that he frequently had to stop and catch his breath, as was quite audible over the air. As the preacher paused his bellowing to gasp for air, Dad and my uncle and I would howl with laughter at this guy. We called him "The Breather." I thought the man was crazy.

My parents were virtuous, but not religious. Both had been baptized, Mom in the Baptist Church and Dad in the Methodist Church. However, the family never went to church. Mom was wary of Christians ("They never do what they say they should do"), while Dad simply thought the whole thing daft.

When I was ten years old or so, my maternal grandmother would take me to her church, where she was a regular parishioner: First Baptist Church, 813 E. Spring Street, New Albany, Indiana. I also went to Sunday School there. I liked the music at the service. We sang all the old Protestant standards: "Softly and Tenderly," "In the Garden," "Just as I Am," "Blessed Assurance," "Amazing Grace," etc. I did not like Sunday School, but I liked the singing. We sang all the time, because our Sunday School teacher (whose name escapes me) played piano, and so our classroom had a piano in it. She didn't so much play it as pound out the chords. My favorite was "Brighten the Corner Where You Are." In my mind I can still see her sitting at that piano, her back to us, pounding out the chords and singing at the top of her lungs, all the while glancing back at us kids (see Burl "Big Daddy" Ives sing a cover of the song on YouTube. Wonderful!).

I was baptized at the First Baptist Church on October 9, 1966. I was twelve years old. Every fall all the twelve-year-olds were herded into the church to hear the pastor's pitch. The pitch was this: Jesus loved you so much that if you didn't believe in him he would send you to everlasting hell. Following this hour-long harangue was the altar call, at which time anyone who wanted to accept Jesus Christ as his or her personal Lord and Savior had to come forward up to the altar (hence, altar call) and say so.

Not wanting to spend eternity in hell, I marched forward. I was the only person who did so that day. The pastor placed his arm around me, and turned me around to face the congregation. The pastor asked me, "Son, do you accept Jesus Christ as your personal Lord and Savior?" I said I did. He then said something to the effect, "This young man has been saved!"

The following Sunday I was baptized. Wearing a pair of blue jean shorts and a white T-shirt over which I wore a white robe, I waded into the baptismal pool that hit me at my waist. The pastor, Rev. McKeny, was already standing in the pool waiting for me. He placed his hand over my face and dunked me backward three times, all the while saying, "I baptize you in the name of the Father, and of the Son, and of the Holy Ghost."

After that I stopped going to church. I convinced my grandmother that since I had been saved, what was the point in my going to church and Sunday School?

I did not return to church until I was eighteen. I did not return out of any hankering for God, though. I returned because Sara Jacoby went to Central Christian Church (Disciples of Christ) and sang in the choir. Ironically, Central was just down Spring Street from First Baptist. I was in love, you see. Sara and I met at New Albany High School. I was seventeen, and she was sixteen. We sang in the high school concert choir. After she and I had been dating for a while, I joined Central so I could see her on Sunday. I sang tenor; she sang soprano.

It was at Central that I got to know Martha Saunders. Ms. Saunders had been my math teacher in the seventh and ninth grades at Hazelwood Junior High (as it was then called), so I was familiar with her. She was also the wife of the pastor at Central. At Central Ms. Saunders and I had these great debates about religion. I was brash; she was patient. I was sarcastic, and she just smiled. Over the next four years we continued these battles, and by the time Sara and I left New Albany to begin our married life on the Bloomington campus of Indiana University (where I was a graduate student first in English and then in library science, and Sara finished her undergraduate degree before attending dental school),

Ms. Saunders had completely turned me around. I was Christian.

During those undergraduate days I went to school full time at Indiana University Southeast, lived at home, and worked part time during the school year and full time during the summer at Nance Floral Shoppe. I drove a delivery van and delivered flowers. Nance Floral Shoppe was, and still is, located at the corner of Eighth and Spring Street in New Albany, across from the former St. Edward Hospital, where I was born.

My job at Nance's was, until my teaching job at Carmel Catholic High School, the most enjoyable job I ever had. My route for delivering flowers was in rural Floyd, Harrison, and Clark Counties. I would load up the truck right after lunch and then head out for places like Sellersburg, Henryville, Charlestown, New Washington, Georgetown, Floyds Knobs, New Salisbury, and Palmyra. I would not return to the shop until late afternoon. All I had to do then was sweep the floor of the workroom where the women arranged the floral decorations.

Cruising down the road was fun, and the people I encountered on the job were always interesting. One of the customers sported bright orange hair (unusual in the years 1972 to 1976), and she swore on a stack of Bibles that a wild bird was loose in her house. She always wanted me to shoo it away. It didn't take me long to figure out that she was a few bricks shy of a full load. So when I came to her place (she ordered flowers for herself weekly), I'd ask for a broom and swish it under her couch. "He's gone," I'd tell her. She was pleased. Then there was the customer who worked at the Sellersburg branch of the floral shop. She was left-handed. When she gave me directions on how to get to a certain house in Sellersburg she would say, "Ok, honey"—she called everybody *honey*—"you turn *right* when you come to the first stop sign, then you turn *left* at the very next street." The problem was that when she said *right* she meant *left*, and when she said *left* she meant *right*, so you had to reverse everything she said.

There were the funeral home cutups at a certain funeral home in New Albany who liked to play bizarre games with a blank gun. One of these games was to burst in on you while you were alone in the back room where the flowers were actually deposited. You would be in there, alone, bringing in the flowers, when all of a sudden the door to the main body of the funeral home would fly open and out would pop one of the funeral home directors brandishing a blank gun and firing away with a maniacal grin. There was the massage parlor above the adult bookstore in Clarksville where I frequently delivered a dozen red roses, *always* with the admonition from the boss that if I wasn't back in thirty minutes I was fired. Mostly, though, I loved being out on the road. I savored the freedom of movement, and I seriously entertained becoming an over-the-road truck driver (so glad I didn't). *Overdrive* magazine was essential reading at this time.

Now one of the duties of this job was that every Saturday I had to place two vases of flowers on the old high altar at St. Mary's Church. The church was located just down the street from the shop. I had no idea what "the old high altar" was, but I was given instruction as to its whereabouts. So I did so every Saturday morning for four years. At first I merely stomped in with vases in hand, plopped them down on the designated spot, and quickly left the place. However, after the first year of doing that, I began taking my time while in the church. I had never seen the inside of a Catholic Church, and St. Mary's looked nothing like First Baptist or Central. What was all that *stuff*? Statues of people all over the place and red candles in metal racks burned seemingly everywhere. Huge paintings adorned the walls on either side of the altar. There was this railing running nearly the width of the church. St. Mary's didn't smell like First Baptist or Central, either. You could smell the candles, of course, but another odor wafted through the air as well. I later learned the odor was incense. After that first year I would place the flowers on their designated spots, and then I would sit down in a pew and gawk.

I wanted to know more about all this. Many of the women who designed the floral arrangements at the shop were Catholic, and so I began peppering them with questions about all this stuff I saw inside St. Mary's Church. Their answers led to more questions from me.

One day, one of the women at the shop brought me a newspaper called *Our Sunday Visitor*. I took it home and devoured it. Reading it was like being bombarded with a new language; a new vocabulary was being presented to me, words such as *liturgy, sacristy, lectionary, thurible*. The next day I asked the woman who had given it to me where I could get more copies of the paper. She told me that issues were often stashed in the narthex of a church (I had to ask her what a narthex was), free for the taking. The following Saturday I headed to the narthex of St. Mary's Church, and sure enough, I found issues of *Our Sunday Visitor*. From that day until my last day of work at the shop in early August 1976, I picked up a copy of that paper every Saturday.

In mid-August 1976, Sara and I headed to the main campus of Indiana University. I was housed in Foley (now demolished), while Sara was in Moffett. My curiosity about Catholicism continued.

Since the women at the floral shop were no longer at hand to answer my questions, I turned to the reference section in the IU library and pulled down the *New Catholic Encyclopedia* for answers. What a wealth of information! I spent hours reading this and that. I would read one entry, and that would lead me to read another entry, and then another entry, and so on. Also in the reference section was a copy of the Douay-Rheims translation of the Bible. What I liked about this was that in the front of the Bible were printed all these Catholic prayers: Hail Mary, Glory Be, Memorare, Confiteor, etc. There was a little section explaining how to pray the rosary. Also, I was fascinated by the names of some of the books of the Old Testament: 1 & 2 Paralipomenon? 1 & 2 Esdras? Those books were not in my KJV!

I began attending Sunday Mass at the nearby St. Charles Borromeo Catholic Church. Scary stuff. Highly self-conscious, worried that I would immediately be spotted as a heretic, and clueless as to what was playing out before me, I parked myself in the very back pew and on the end (for a quick getaway if things got too overwhelming, as they did at first). I simply did what everybody else did around me: when they stood, I stood; when they knelt, I knelt.

One Sunday on leaving Mass I passed the bulletin board, and a flyer tacked up there caught my eye. The flyer said that a "schola" of monks from St. Meinrad Archabbey would be giving a free concert at St. Charles. Free. All welcome.

I went. St. Charles was packed. Even saw some of my professors there from IU. The concert was in the evening. A group of four to five monks, in habit, chanted medieval Gregorian chant. Blew me away! Never heard anything like that at First Baptist or Central! My resolve to join the Catholic Church only grew stronger after that concert.

I talked it over with Sara. She didn't have any problems with my joining the Catholic Church but asked that I wait to do so until after our wedding on the day after Christmas. That made sense to me.

Soon after returning to campus following our wedding I contacted St. Charles and told the pastor I wanted to join the Catholic Church. In January 1977 I began meeting with a priest to do just that.

The priest's name was Fr. Charles Fisher, but he asked to be addressed as Fr. Chuck. Fr. Chuck was the associate pastor at St. Charles. He was the first priest I had ever seen with a beard. I was the only man in the group of no more than ten. All the women in the group were coming into the Catholic Church in order to marry Catholic men.

We met weekly. Our textbook was Anthony J. Wilhelm's *Christ Among Us*. I cannot recall a lesson. I very well remember, though, Fr. Chuck's singing voice. One of the best voices I've ever heard in a priest. He sang the Mass beautifully.

A few weeks before Easter I made my first confession to Fr. Bob Borchertmeyer, the pastor. I was terrified, but Fr. Bob walked me through it.

I was received into the Catholic Church on Easter Sunday, April 10, 1977. The Mass was at six in the morning. Sara, both her parents, and her two sisters attended the Mass. Molly Mills, a friend of Sara's sister, was my sponsor. The morning was quite cool, but the afternoon was bright and warm. We all walked around campus later that day after lunch.

I have finished eating breakfast down in the dining room of New Melleray Abbey. The long night of prayer is over, so I head up to my room and change from my choir clothes (nicer clothes that I wear down in the chapel) into a pair of shorts. I snatch up my psalter, and I go back down the stairs and step outside. Warm, bright, and not too humid. A good day to be out in the garden!

I begin walking down the monastery driveway. At the base of the drive I cross the two-lane road that runs in front of the monastery and enter the driveway to Holy Family Church, which is right across the street from the monastery. The church sits about a hundred and fifty yards back from the road. Two rows of mature pines line the mowed yard that leads up to the church. I like to approach the church by walking up between those two rows of pines. Kind of like a cloister feeling.

When I reach the church, I walk to the back of it. Then, to the west, a rolling field of corn opens up. The green of the cornfield meets the blue horizon of the sky in the far distance. The air smells green. Very quiet. The only sound is a passing car on the nearby road and the rustling of the leaves of corn from the light breeze. At this time of year the corn is only about sixteen inches tall.

I love this scene. The field has alternated between corn, soybeans, and just plain grass over the years that I've been coming here, but the view always inspires me. The view begs for prayer, for it is filled with God. Hence the psalter I brought along with me. I open the psalter (*The Psalms, A New Transla-tion: Singing Version*) and begin where I left off: Psalm 61. For the next few minutes I pray five psalms over the fields.

When I finish the five psalms I just stand and stare at the sight. Back in August 2011 I stood at this same spot. Someone was driving a big green farm machine that day that mowed the tall grass and weeds of the field. Perhaps all that mowed grass was later gathered into those huge rolls that dot farm fields, but that is just a guess. Anyway, the machine would drive near to where I stood and then turn in a tight circle and head out the other way. The machine did not follow a straight line but curved slightly west in a large sweep, and all the while it did so, the machine slowly climbed a gentle hill. When the machine reached the crest of the hill I saw it turn north, and after that it faded out of sight. I would estimate that the point at which the machine disappeared from view was about a half a mile from where I stood. A few minutes later, without my being able to hear any noise, the machine would reappear and slowly make its way back to me.

All this was a beautiful sight, especially when the machine was moving away from me and was at a great distance from me. The machine was a bright green dot in the sea of grass and the bright blue sky. When it had been near, the machine roared with great power, but the noise lessened as the machine lum-bered away from me. But the beauty was not just in what I could see or hear. The beauty was also in the loneliness the scene instilled in me. It was lonely watching the machine when it was at a great distance. I could see it but barely hear it. When it was near me, I could see the man in the cab operating the big machine, and he would wave. I would return his wave. But when the machine turned and began lumbering away, I would ask myself: Who was that operating that machine? Was he a neighboring farmer? How did that machine get to this field?

But then I thought: From the vantage point of the man op-erating the machine, he doesn't feel the loneliness. He doesn't feel the separation. The man operating the machine seeks only the goal for which he is there: to mow the field.

From my vantage point, though, standing at the edge of that field, the feeling of loneliness was very real. Why? I don't know. I can't explain it. I only know that I experienced it. Nor can I explain why the whole thing fascinated me.

I awaken from my reverie with a jolt. I look at my watch: eight forty-five. I need to get back to my room; Terce is thirty minutes away. I spin around and make a brisk walk back to the monastery. I've been here one day now. Four more days remain. I pray that I will make this time of prayer fruitful.

About a forty-five-minute talk with Br. Paul after Terce. He caught me in the cloister as I was leaving the chapel. We started off talking there but soon moved to a couple of chairs in the gift shop. He always fills me in on stuff in which I am interested: what's new in the house, where he has traveled lately, situation down at Ava, etc. Today he wants to know if I would be willing to review the second edition of Maxwell Johnson's *Benedictine Daily Prayer*. Oh, yeah!

Br. Paul is very calm. He's quite measured in speech. However, he laughs and makes droll observations. I cannot, though, recall ever having a conversation with him in which he raised his voice either in excitement or anger. He's even-steven.

Unlike the subprior. He is spontaneous, flip, and earthy. He tells wonderful stories. I once met him for a summer conference at the University of St. Mary of the Lake in Mundelein, Illinois, the seminary for the Archdiocese of Chicago. Since the seminary is directly across the street from the school at which I teach, I was more than happy to be with him at this conference.

It just so happened that a colleague of mine in the department of religion was attending this same conference, so the three of us sat together. The subprior was assiduously taking notes. Afterward, a light reception was offered. At this reception the three of us enjoyed our refreshments, and the subprior blasted off on a wide variety of topics, both those covered in the conference we had just attended and other subjects both ecclesiastical and civil.

The subprior was bobbing and weaving, tagging topics one after another, in a rapid-fire manner, and he was right on the money about them too. Making this all the more spectacular was his physical appearance. He is a tall, lanky fellow with a large wingspan. So when he gets going and he waves those arms and he punctuates the end of his sentences with "yeah, yeah," you notice him. He wears black-framed glasses, and they tend to stand out against his salt-and-pepper beard. He gets your attention.

My colleague was agog.

There's something else about the subprior that can leave one agog: the man can sing. You know how I said that Fr. Chuck had one of the best voices I ever heard in a priest? The subprior is better. It's no accident that he frequently cantors in choir. I once complimented him on his singing. He bounced back immediately with, "Buy my CD?"

Departure day; always busy. Clean the room in the Monastic Center. Go down to the room just outside the Monastic Center where the linens are stored and fetch fresh sheets and towels. Sometimes, especially if Hal is in the Monastic Center as well, mop the hall. Pack up everything. Lug it all down three flights of stairs. Stash it all in the trunk of the car. Just as when you were a kid, getting to the vacation destination was all exciting and fun, while the return trip home was a drag, so it is when leaving the Monastic Center.

I jump in the car and fire it up. I take a last look at the place. Next year, 2017, will be my twentieth consecutive year at New Melleray.

"Next year, New Melleray," I say to no one. I slip the gearshift into drive and bug out for my three-hour tour home.

Abbey of Gethsemani

Driving south out of Louisville, Kentucky, on I-65. Two miles south of I-265 (the Gene Snyder Freeway), on your right, you will notice a small bland white sign with black letters. If you're not looking for it, you will blow right past it. The sign reads

---

Antioch
Old Regular Baptist Church of Jesus Christ

Every time I drive down to my destination in central Kentucky I look for that sign. It always cracks me up.[1] Plus, I know I'm close to my destination when I see that sign.

Let's break down the name of that church. Antioch: the place where the followers of Jesus were first called Christians. Old: this church is not new, and it has a tradition. Regular: because it is old, and because it is named after the location where followers of Jesus were first called Christians. This particular church is linked to a way of life that has been tested, a way of life that is not based on the cool or the hipsters, but on the covenant. And is it really necessary to insert the word *Baptist* in the title of the church? Isn't doing so being redundant?

Someday I *must* stop and see this church.

---

[1] One might conclude from glancing at the sign (especially when you're driving seventy mph and see the sign unexpectedly) that this particular Baptist church is *regular* in the sense of being a fixed, uniform entity. That is certainly how I interpreted the sign until I learned of the Christian denomination called Regular Baptist Churches.

But not today.

No, today I'm heading for a place that is old. Old in the sense that it was founded in 1848, but old also in the sense that this place is connected to a group of people that stretches back all the way to 1098.

No, today I'm heading for a place that is regular. Every day is the same; the schedule of the place is the epitome of regular. Just as a person drags a pencil along the straight edge of a yardstick in order to maintain a straight line, so the men who live at the place where I'm heading use a rule to lay out the plan of their life. That rule is known as the Rule of Saint Benedict, and the men at the place where I'm heading are known as Cistercians. These Cistercians, like the Cistercians at New Melleray, have been following the Rule of Saint Benedict since the founders of the Cistercians left the Benedictine abbey of Molesme back in the eleventh century.

Today, Friday, July 22, 2016, I'm driving down to the Abbey of Gethsemani.

Two blinking eyes. That is what the flashing traffic signal lights look like to me, two blinking eyes. And these blinking eyes are at the intersection of Kentucky Highway 247 and the entrance to the monastery. If you're traveling on Hwy 247, in either direction, you see the yellow blinking eyes. If you're leaving the monastery, you see the red eyes.

Now, during the day these blinking lights are noticeable, but certainly not interesting. Yeah, you see them as you approach them, that driving instructor in your brain acknowledges them, but frankly those blinking eyes just don't register. At night, though, especially after Vigils (which starts at a quarter past three in the morning), when you step outside the abbey church to prolong the prayer of choir and perhaps catch some fresh air, the blinking eyes, which are clearly visible from the avenue in front of the monastery, are mysterious and—I know this will sound odd—somewhat frightening. I mean, Hwy 247 is not a busy highway. It is even more lonely in the darkness of a three-forty-five morning. Hardly anyone is out and about, maybe you and another retreatant, there in the front avenue, looking up at the sea of stars. The occasional car that does pass by seems out of place and time, not to mention intrusive. You hear the whining of the tires long before you see the headlights of the car. Then it rushes past you, and you try to see the invisible driver, but you can't, and all that remains is the waning whine of the tires and the taillights flickering out of sight. And with your prayers and hopes and dreams having been lifted up to the Lord in the predawn morn as you walked along that front avenue, you go back into the guesthouse. But those red and yellow blinking eyes? They're still there. Watching. Ever watching. They never stop blinking. It's as though the blinking eyes are giving us a warning, and not just a traffic warning. What is that warning? I don't know.

I drive into the front avenue, having driven beneath the blinking eyes, and park across from the gift shop.

I step out of my air-conditioned car, and I am slammed by the Big Heat and his good friend Mr. Humidity. To make matters worse, the huge front lawn in the front avenue is being mowed, and the combination of freshly mowed grass wafting through the air along with the Big Heat and his good friend Mr. Humidity makes breathing a challenge. More about that later, though.

I walk to the guesthouse. No one is at the desk. However, there is a handwritten sign that reads

> *To check in,*
> *Please call 178 or 129.*

To the right of the sign is the phone. Do I have to dial nine to get out? I don't know. So I just dial 178. No answer. I disconnect and dial 129. I get the answering machine. "My name is Mark," I say to the machine. "I'd like to check in." I hang up.

About three minutes later here comes a monk. "You Mark?" he asks.

"Yes," I answer.

"Last name?" he asks sitting down at the desk.

"Plaiss," and I spell it.

The monk unfolds a paper resting on the desk. The paper has names listed on it. He scans the paper. He looks some more.

"How do you spell that?"

I spell it out again, emphasizing the "P" of my last name. "P as in Paul," I tell him.

"Oh, P," said the monk. "I thought your name started with F."

He finds my name. Looking up from the sheet he asks, "What room do you want?"

"Third floor is fine."

He writes 303 next to my name and hands me the keys. "Where are you from, Mark?" the monk asks me.

"Fox Lake, Illinois."

"Did you come straight from there?"

"I did."

"How long was that?"

"Seven hours. Four hundred miles."

"Have you been here before?" he asks.

Let's start with the last time I was here, which was about two years before this retreat. And because that last retreat involved the Big Heat and his good friend Mr. Humidity, let's get back to them too.

The last time I was here I was housed in the South Wing of the monastery, where there is no air-conditioning. Let me give you an example of the degree to which the Big Heat and Mr. Humidity dig in their heels during high summer here in central Kentucky: the temperature in my room was at least a hundred degrees. I know this, because a thermometer was tacked to the white brick wall just opposite the door to my room. The red line of that thermometer stood at one hundred. Question: What wag tacked that thermometer there?!

You take a lot of cold showers when you sit in a room where the temperature is one hundred degrees. In order to do that, though, I had to walk down the hall to where the toilets and showers were located. You see, in the South Wing of the monastery, where male guests can be housed, the rooms have no toilet and shower. There is a sink, but toilet and shower are down the hall. So a few times a day I trudged down the hall in shorts and flip-flops with a towel slung over my left shoulder.

When you enter this area, though, the heat and the humidity move from oppressive to brutal. An open window in the room mocked me. Really, an open window is expected to bring relief? You needed gills to breathe!

Finally, the angry sun set. The room, though, was still an oven. The fan, which I set right next to my bed and pointed right at me as I lay naked atop the sheets, whirled. The insects and frogs outside sang. Sleep? Forget it. How can you sleep in this soup? Doze, yes; sleep, no. So every once in a while when my dozing died, I stepped over to the sink and splashed cold water on my face. I placed a washcloth under the cold water, wrung it out, and placed it on the back of my neck.

I glanced at the clock as I trudged back to bed: ten thirty. I had been in bed since after Compline, which ended around 7:50 p.m. At least now it was dark outside. When I hit the hay upon returning to my cell from Compline, light still filled the sky.

I lay in bed sweating, and I thought: These monks do this every summer for their entire *lives*?

Occasionally, a car passed by on Hwy 247. Then, nothing. Except the waiting.

I glanced at the clock. The red numbers told me that Vigils would blast off in four hours and fifteen minutes.

The Big Heat.

My first time here was quite different.

In the summer of 1977, I was a first-year graduate student at Indiana University in Bloomington. I was working on my master's degree in English, though by the end of that first semester of graduate school I would switch to the School of Library Science.

Anyway, in the summer of 1977 I was newly married. My bride and I were living in married housing on campus, an apartment without air-conditioning. So one blazing hot afternoon, in a desperate ploy to beat the heat, I walked the mile from married housing to the library—which was air-conditioned.

Having no pressing classwork, I decided to browse the stacks. I soon found myself on the floor of the ten-story library where the books on religion were shelved. I was not looking for anything in particular, nor was I hunting for any given topic in religion. I was merely browsing.

Making my way through the stacks I came across a blue cloth-covered hardback book. I pulled the book from the shelf and flipped through the pages. I landed on a black-and-white photograph of a large white barn. Several men in dark robes were sitting on benches in front of this barn. These men, I realized, were monks. They were sitting with their hands folded in their laps and their heads bowed, the hoods of their robes up over their heads. For some reason I inferred that the men were bowing their heads not so much in prayer as in obedience or even fear. Standing at the door of the barn were two monks in white robes. It appeared to me as though these two monks were in conversation. They were facing one another and gesturing with their hands. My first reaction on seeing this photograph was to wonder what these monks were doing in front of a barn.

I continued leafing through the book. I discovered a daily schedule the monks followed. They rose at two o'clock in the morning and went to bed at seven thirty in the evening. Between those times the monks worked and came together periodically for "offices" bearing odd titles: Matins, Lauds, Prime, Terce, Sext, None, Vespers, Compline. In the book I saw more black-and-white photographs: a monk operating a bulldozer, monks making a deep bow while standing in choir stalls, a monk celebrating Mass. For someone who was raised and baptized in the Baptist Church and who had been received into the Catholic Church just the previous Easter, all of this was strange stuff. Here was the clincher, though. From leafing through the book I learned that the person who wrote this book had been a monk in a monastery in nearby Kentucky.

Where was this monastery?

I was intrigued. I brought the book downstairs, checked it out, and carried it home. Walking back to the apartment I could not help scanning the pages. For the next couple of weeks I carried the book with me to my classes. When classes grew dull—and what graduate class is not sometimes riddled with ennui?—I delved into monkdom. I showed the book to some of my classmates. No one was interested.

The book was *The Waters of Siloe* by Thomas Merton.

The irony was that I had been born and raised within an hour's drive of Merton and his monastery, but I never heard of him or the Abbey of Gethsemani until I was twenty-three years old and in graduate school.

My hometown, New Albany, Indiana, sits on the north bank of the Ohio River opposite Louisville, Kentucky. After moving to Bloomington, my wife and I made frequent weekend trips back to New Albany. On one of those trips I decided I needed to find this monastery.

My wife was not keen on the idea of visiting a monastery and seeing a bunch of monks. So my two younger brothers volunteered to go with me. At the last moment my grandmother, my mother's mother, decided she wanted to come along as well. Having been born near Bardstown, Kentucky, she was lured into the trip not from curiosity about the monastery or monks but by the fact that we would be traveling through Bardstown in order to get to the monastery. She would be seeing familiar territory.

An hour later I was coasting to a stop along the avenue of trees lining the driveway at Gethsemani. As I stepped out of the car I was immediately struck by the silence. Slamming the car doors shut seemed an intrusion. But who was I intruding upon? Nobody was in sight.

We followed the signs pointing the way to the abbey church. After we climbed some stairs our journey ended when we opened a door leading into the balcony that overlooked the church.

We stepped to the railing. The long narrow nave seemed to go on and on. Choir stalls were rather near to where we were, but the altar seemed far away down at the opposite end in the apse. The walls were bare whitewashed brick, and the wooden beams supporting the roof were exposed and brown with age. The only religious image I could see was an image of the Blessed Mother at the north end of the west choir. My first impression was that the interior of the church on which I was looking bore no resemblance to the photograph of this same church that was in Merton's *The Waters of Siloe.*

The church was empty that afternoon except for a lone monk. This monk knelt, not in the choir stalls but on the floor between the east and west choir stalls. His back was to us, and he was facing the altar. For what seemed like several minutes my grandmother, brothers, and I stood at the railing of the balcony and watched that lone monk move not a muscle.

It was at this point that my grandmother, a staunch Baptist, began peppering me with questions. She was trying to whisper these questions to me, but was failing miserably: "Is that a monk? Why is he here all alone? Aren't there others? Why is he kneeling there like that?" Her whispers seemed to ricochet off those whitewashed brick walls.

Since Vespers was well over an hour away, I decided it would be best to drive the twelve miles back to Bardstown, get a bite to eat, and then return for Vespers. During that time I could answer my grandmother's questions, and that poor monk could pray in peace.

So that is what we did.

About an hour later we returned to the monastery. We climbed back up the stairs to the balcony. I was relieved when the balcony was empty. I was anticipating answering questions my grand-mother would have when Vespers cranked up. I would not be disturbing anyone when I answered her questions.

We once again approached the railing of the balcony to look out over the church. Down below that same monk was still there, in the exact same position. It appeared to us that he had not moved an inch since we last saw him. And once again, he was all alone down there.

"Why, Mark, he's still *there*!" my grandmother cried. Her voice rolled like thunder down the long narrow nave.

To that monk's credit, he didn't move. He didn't even flinch.

But that was enough for me. I spun around and headed for the door, my brothers right behind me. Bringing up the rear was my grandmother, all agog about the motionless monk.

That monk might not have moved, but I would have loved to have seen his face.

Fortunately, this time I am not housed in the South Wing, but in the guesthouse, with an air conditioner in good working order. I firmly believe that air-conditioning is one of the great-est inventions of the twentieth century.

It's good to be back here. My first office is Sext. A stack of psalters sits on a desk in the back of the guest area. A sign on the desk lists the psalms to be sung for the Little Hours. I pick up the psalter and find a chair. The guest area is situated be-hind a small iron railing that is approximately three and a half feet high and runs the width of the church. In the middle of the railing is a gate that swings open so the guests can move up toward the altar when Mass is celebrated and to receive the blessing of the abbot at the conclusion of Compline. The choir stalls are just a few feet away from this railing. About twelve people, mostly women, are present in the guest area.

I watch the monks file in. I recognize some of them: Quenon, Connor, Luke, Dietz. I recognize other faces, but don't know their names. I see there are two postulants and one novice. One young man is in street clothes. Observer? Of those monks I

recognize, their faces appear more drawn. Other monks I've
seen over the years walk far more slowly than they once did.

The face I miss the most is Kelty's.

Father Matthew Kelty, who died in 2011, was a favorite here.
He gave talks after Compline. What a joy to hear! Right after
Compline he slipped into the guest chapel adjacent to the
church and talked to anyone who cared to listen. He'd waddle
in, usually with a pile of books in his arms. He wouldn't exactly
slam the books down on the ambo, but he always seemed to
put them down smartly. He was a short man and stout. His
thin white hair covered a head that seemed littered with moles.
He had a quick grin—a mischievous one, really—and his eyes
danced with joy. I don't think I ever saw him morose. His voice
betrayed his Boston heritage, and it contrasted acutely with
the Kentucky twang. Just hearing him read was a delight. He
seemed to know instinctively what words to punch or drag
out or cut short.

He'd talk about anything. Read anything. Comment on
whatever seemed to flash through his mind. Sometimes he
would read from the newspaper. He was fond of poetry, so he
would often read poems and make little comments about them.
Then he would shuffle through his pile of stuff, and on finding
an item he'd say, "Here's something," and he would read it
and then riff on that. Since you were right there in front of him,
his style was informal. This was no lecture. Frequently, the
audience would chuckle at his comments. It wasn't really con-
versational, either, but he gave you the illusion that *you* were
having a conversation with *him*. This went on for twenty or
thirty minutes. I guarantee you, no one was ever bored. People
hung on his every word.

His genius here was that *whatever* he talked about, he swung
it around to the guest, to the retreat, to that particular weekend
or week, and he showed the guests how God was fitting into
that picture.

I spoke with him exactly twice. Back in the mid-1990s I was on retreat here, and I stopped by his office in the guesthouse. The desk in his office was piled with books and papers. More books and papers were strewn about the office: on chairs, bookshelves, floor, or windowsill—wherever there was room. The only chair not filled with books and papers was for the guest. I sat there. We chatted briefly, perhaps fifteen minutes. He asked where I was from, had I been there before, etc. I told him I enjoyed his post-Compline talks.

The last time I spoke with him was just two or three years before he died. I spoke only two words to him. I walked into the guesthouse one morning, and he was manning the desk. The phone was ringing, a guest was talking to him, and Fr. Kelty was trying to give his attention to both but failing. As I approached the desk, he was trying to answer the phone. A red light was flashing on the phone console, and Fr. Kelty, with phone receiver at his ear, was saying *hello* repeatedly. Frustrated, he looked up, saw me, and asked, "Do *you* know how to work this thing?!"

"I'll try," I answered.

I took the phone receiver from him, looked down at the console and pushed the flashing red button. "Hello?" I heard a voice say on the other end.

I handed the receiver to Fr. Kelty who was speaking to the other guest. Without missing a beat in his speech he said, "Guesthouse," into the phone.

Many of his post-Compline talks have been compiled into a book.[2] They make good reading. You had to have heard him deliver the talks, though, to really appreciate the words, and you would have to have seen him flash that smile in order to understand the impact of what was going on: he was making God present to us.

---

[2] Matthew Kelty, *My Song Is of Mercy* (Kansas City, MO: Sheed & Ward, 1994).

Vigils Saturday morning is recited by different readers from the ambo. Except for the light at the ambo, all the lights in the church are extinguished during both nocturns. I'd say eight of us guests are present.

At the conclusion of Vigils I remain seated in the guest area. The lights, having been turned back on at the dismissal, are quickly snapped off. I don't remain there long, though.

I step outside and walk up to the front avenue. A full moon, ringed by a halo of haze, hangs in the sky. Insects sing. A bat flitters about. Dew drips from the guests' cars parked there.

My intention is to circle the drive; however, a monk has beat me out there. He notices me, and he confines himself to that portion of the drive closest to the highway, while I stay on the drive closest to the gift shop. A kind of unspoken gentlemen's agreement for privacy.

I walk back and forth on the, oh, fifty-yard or so length of driveway. I recite psalms, but not for long. In this silence and in this darkness words are superfluous. What is required is listening.

Lightning flashes to the north, but since I never hear thunder, the storm must be far away, maybe over Louisville or even southern Indiana. A car rushes by on the highway. A cow moos. Then nothing. Just the sound of God enveloping the darkness, which isn't dark for him at all.

> *O God, you are my God, for you I long;*
> *for you my soul is thirsting.*

Night, especially predawn night, brings out my humility, O Lord. The moon and stars that you have splashed across the sky enforce my sense of insignificance and lowliness.

Yet at the same time night draws me closer to you, O God. Your presence is almost palpable. Prayer oozes out of me. Is this because the darkness hides the distractions? Does the night paint your face and so make you visible to us?

At night it is easy to lift up my hands to you, O Lord. My soul swoons sweetly at that hour. So when light shines, and the objects of this world are clear and sharp, help me, O God, to recall your face and to remember that you are still with me amid the woo and coo of day. Amen.

Those eyes, those red and yellow eyes, are blinking.

The Spirit moves as he will, especially my encounter with the Holy Spirit here at Gethsemani in mid-September 1995 and early October 1996. The 1995 weekend retreat was my first retreat here. On the first day of my retreat in 1995, between Terce and Sext, I walked up the hill opposite the front avenue, the hill with the statue of Joseph holding baby Jesus. It was an overcast day, humid, but with a nice breeze. I looked out over the countryside. I liked the way Hwy 247 meandered through the surrounding knobs, and I enjoyed watching the occasional car snake its way along the highway and then disappear.

I descended the hill and walked back to the church. It was a few minutes after eleven, so I had approximately an hour and fifteen minutes before Sext was prayed.

I stepped into the church: no monks and no guests. I sat down in the metal chair. I was alone. I don't even recall anyone sticking a head in the door to take a peek at the place.

But not alone. Perhaps thirty minutes went by as I just listened to the silence. Suddenly I felt a presence, that God was right there with me, *next* to me. This consciousness of God's presence was immediate; in other words, there was no gradual buildup of my awareness of God's presence. It was *boom*, and he was there. My breathing grew rapid. Fear struck my gut. My eyes were wide open. The fear, though, died. I felt as if I were being overshadowed. I felt awe and wonder.

Then, just as quickly as this phenomenon pounced on me, it left me. I looked around, twisting my body so I could get a good view of all angles. Nothing. No one. I have never experienced anything like that again.

In early October 1996 I was back at Gethsemani, this time for the five-day retreat. When I came down to the church for Vigils on Wednesday of that week, the church was completely dark. Well, the vigil lamp near the tabernacle down at the far end of the church was burning, but that was it. No one was in the guest area.

I felt my way to a chair (didn't scrape into one!) and sat down. I had left my room at 2:57, so I figured I had about fifteen minutes before Vigils blasted off. I settled in and looked around, actually, *listened* around. Couldn't hear a thing. Not a cough or a sniff or rustle of cowls.

Where were those guys?

I soon found out. About five minutes after I landed in my seat the lights flipped on. Those guys were already in their stalls!

Only one of the six psalms that morning was sung; the remaining psalms were recited. I liked that. Singing at three fifteen in the morning is not easy.

So Vigils ended, and I decided to stay put in my chair there in the guest area. The monks dribbled out of the church. Forty minutes or so after the conclusion of Vigils the door to my left opened (the door that leads to the sacristy), and out stepped a monk without his cowl. He had the hood of his scapular up over his head, so I could not see his face. Neither on the retreat the previous year nor during this retreat up to this point had I seen a monk with the hood up.

Anyway, this monk walked very quickly through the door. He had rosary beads in his hands. He approached the gate that separates the guest area from the rest of the church, walked through it, and sat down right behind me. I was a little freaked out about this. This monk had the whole monastery in which to pray, plus something like two thousand acres of monastery forest to frolic in, and he sat right behind me in the guest area where there were no other guests present?

Do I stay or vamoose, I asked myself. I stayed.

So I'm sitting there in the dark, with this monk behind me. No way I can pray now; I'm too self-conscious. As I sit there staring straight ahead and trying to figure this whole thing out, I notice that the doors of the gate through which the monk had walked in were open. He had failed to close them. At that precise moment when I became cognizant of the open gate I heard the monk behind me whisper, "Not now." Then, he bolted away, leaving the church from the doors behind us.

What the hell was that?

Later, after None, in an effort to shake off that bizarre episode, I snatched up my psalter and headed for the hills on the west side of the highway that runs by the monastery. I passed under the blinking eyes and crossed the highway. I remained on the asphalt road until it became a gravel road, and I stayed on the gravel road until it became a dirt path, and I continued on the dirt path until it dissolved into a path through weeds. I hiked back what seemed to me a long way. I walked as far as I could in a field that ended at a dense wood. This spot was at the top of a small hill, more like a rise. Along the path in the weeds I had come across one of those old wooden meditation chairs, and I had dragged it with me across that field. Now I plopped that chair down, turned the chair so I could see where I had just walked, sat down, and took it all in.

The October sky was bright and blue. I could barely make out the tops of the old silos in the distance. Hawks circled above me, gliding effortlessly. Crickets and grasshoppers flittered about. A breeze rustled the tall grass before me. I could no longer hear traffic over on Hwy 247; nor could I hear the bells from the monastery. Sublime, all so sublime. So I did what was called for at that moment. I pulled out my psalter and prayed.

Two of the most important retreats of my life.

Except for perhaps another, and it was here at Gethsemani.

In early August 2006 I was back here at Gethsemani with my younger son, John, then fifteen years old. Walking down the hall of the guesthouse after Lauds one morning, I heard someone say, "You must be a Plaiss." I turned around to see who had said that, and I was looking into the face of a monk. I pegged him to be in his early sixties or so.

"I'm Mark," I said extending my hand. "How do you know me?" And the monk and I shook hands.

"You must be Mike Plaiss's brother," he replied, "You look just like him."

"I am," I said.

My brother Mike and this monk, the guestmaster, had become friends via their respective interest in astronomy. Mike had spoken of him to me before. Mike was a past president of the Louisville Astronomical Society. Mike had brought his telescope out to Gethsemani in order to escape the light pollution of the Louisville area.

Since the guestmaster and I were standing in the middle of the hallway of the guesthouse having this conversation, we decided our talking there was not a good idea. So we agreed to get together later that afternoon.

We met at five o'clock in his office in the guesthouse. I was wearing a T-shirt bearing the logo of the Catholic Theological Union, and he asked me about that. I told him I was a graduate of the school.

"Do you know Steve Bevans?" he asked me.

I told him Steve had been my academic advisor while I was a student there and that Steve was also one of three members of my comps board for my MA in theology. The guestmaster said he had been an SVD (Divine Word) before he came to Gethsemani in 1974.

As five fifteen drew near he asked, "Would you and your son care to come to choir for one of the Offices?"

I quickly accepted this unexpected offer.

"How about tomorrow night at Compline?"

I told him that was fine. Feeling bold I asked, "Would it be possible for my son and me to see Merton's hermitage?"

He said nothing, but picked up the phone and dialed. A brief conversation with someone, and he hung up. "That won't be a problem," he said. "No one has been up there all week. I'll pick you and John up out front at nine o'clock tomorrow morning."

John and I were out front at eight forty-five. Just as the tone of the last ring of the nine o'clock chime tolled in the bell tower, a gray pickup truck pulled through the gate at the far end of the driveway. We were about to be picked up.

We drove behind the buildings and down a narrow gravel road. This road intersected with the gravel road that empties out onto Hwy 247 just up from the blinking eyes. We turned right. Immediately we saw a man walking toward us on the gravel road. When the truck approached him, we stopped and the guestmaster introduced us. He was a monk who would be spending the upcoming week at the hermitage, but he wouldn't settle in until that night. Our host told the monk that I had been making retreats at Gethsemani for years and that I was a big Merton fan. He went on to say that he was driving John and me out to the hermitage so we could see it. The monk told him, "Don't forget to lock up!"

We continued driving a short way on the gravel road, and then we turned left. Immediately the familiar front porch of the hermitage swung into view. I'd say we were seventy-five to a hundred yards from the place. The truck stopped on the side of the house where the pile of firewood was stacked. John and I stepped out of the truck and followed the guestmaster to the front door. We walked in, and I recognized the fireplace and the entire front room from the photographs of the place I had seen. Three books were stacked on the large wood desk that was up against the front window. I noticed the oriental artwork that was hung near the front door.

We walked into the kitchen. Off the kitchen was the bedroom. John and I made an about-face and stepped into the chapel. The small room with the shower and toilet was next to the chapel.

The guestmaster took a photograph of me sitting in the rocking chair in the front room. He also took a photograph of John and me standing on the front porch. Finally, he took a photograph of me standing on the porch, leaning on my outstretched arm up against the post on the porch. We were probably there all of ten minutes.

That evening John and I met the guestmaster in front of the door in the guesthouse that leads to the sacristy. John and I followed him through that door and into the choir. We were in the front row of stalls in the north choir on the west end. In fact, John was in the last stall, I was next to John, and the guestmaster was next to me. When we arrived, we didn't even have time to sit. The bell rang, and we turned to our left to face the altar.

What I noticed immediately was that the distance between the north and south choir there at Gethsemani seemed shorter than the distance between the north and south choirs at New Melleray. Compline passed so quickly! In no time it seemed we were receiving the blessing from the abbot.

So I've sung psalms in two monastic choirs having never ever been a monk. How cool is that!

I have brought along something on this retreat that I have never brought along before. I fact, it would not even have occurred to me to pack it. I've got six beers iced down in the cooler.

> *Monastic area*
> *Do not enter*

That sign is posted everywhere here at Gethsemani. Okay, that's not true. But the sign is certainly in several different spots. It just *seems* as if it is everywhere. It's on the wood door in the enclosure wall near the parking lot, for example. Down on the path where the Stations of the Cross are located for use by guests, the sign appears up close to the east end of the church. There at the head of the driveway the sign appears on the gate.

The sign aggravates me.

Intellectually, I understand its purpose. The monks don't want guests butting in on their private family space. That makes perfect sense. I can understand that. Furthermore,

Terrence Kardong is correct when he writes, "Monasteries that are overrun by guests need to protect their monks from the curious; no one comes to the monastery to live in a goldfish bowl or to be part of a theme park."[3]

At our house in Illinois we allow guests in our house, but not in certain sections of it. Same thing goes for the monks. They allow us into their home (witness the guestmaster), but not to all of it.

Having said that, though, the sign still irritates me.

Another irritant? The sign on the floor in the guest area of the church at the gate: "Do Not Go Beyond This Point," reads the sign.

Really?

Why the irritation? It is as though there is something about our religion beyond those signs that is being hidden from the rest of us. Some secret knowledge, some better access to God that we non-monks can't know. For my wife the iron railing that separates the guest area from the remainder of the church is an insult. "I'm not worthy to go beyond a certain point in a church?" Again, intellectually I know all that's not true.

It's not just Gethsemani. New Melleray has the same setup as well.

I don't know, perhaps it's just sour grapes on my part. New Melleray and Gethsemani have bent over backward to accommodate guests. They fulfill Benedict's command to treat all guests as Christ (RB 53).

I need to just get over it. Besides, would you want Silent Stan stomping around your place?

Departure day.

Weekend retreats here at Gethsemani end on Monday morning at eight o'clock, but I'm leaving here Sunday after the ten-thirty Mass. When I was dragging my stuff back out to the car I took notice of the license plates of the cars in the parking lot.

---

[3] Terrence Kardong, *Benedict's Rule: A Translation and Commentary* (Collegeville, MN: Liturgical Press, 1996), 430.

I'm always amazed at the distances people drive to experience Gethsemani. Folks here this weekend are from Indiana, Ohio, Illinois, Colorado, Texas, Tennessee, Alabama, and, of course, Kentucky.

After stashing my stuff in the car, I head back to the guest-house. I climb the steps up to the first floor (the first floor of the guesthouse is *not* the ground floor) to the guestmaster's office. I want to thank Fr. Seamus, the current guestmaster, for housing me in the guesthouse.

Fr. Seamus picks up a sheet of paper that has a list of the persons making retreat the upcoming week. He holds up the sheet and says, "Every room in the South Wing is reserved next week. Some of these men don't know what they're getting into, but most of them do."

I just shake my head.

"A bishop is coming next week," says Fr. Seamus. "He always requests the South Wing. He says he works in air-conditioning and lives in air-conditioning. He says it won't hurt him to live as most of humanity does for just a weekend: without air-conditioning."

The heat index that upcoming week was forecast to be in the triple digits.

Saint Meinrad Archabbey

I'm convinced that the best approach to Saint Meinrad Arch-abbey is from the east. No, not along I-64, but along Indiana Highway 62. Pick up Hwy 62 at Corydon, no farther than Leavenworth. But when you are in Leavenworth, stop at the Overlook Restaurant. The place sits atop a cliff that overlooks (hence the name of the place) the Ohio River at a horseshoe bend in the river. The Indiana side of the river is quite hilly, while across the river the Kentucky side is flat.

If you don't eat at the restaurant, pull into the parking lot and take in the vista. If you are lucky, you will see far below you a barge negotiating the horseshoe bend in the river. If you are really lucky, you will see two barges, one going down-stream (from your left to your right), and the other plowing upstream (from your right to your left), and meeting at the horseshoe bend. Only one passes through the curve at a time. It's fun to watch how they do that.

Eagles sail high above the river. Many times I have sat there for several minutes watching them drift along without ever flapping their wings. Just showing off. You can hear them screech.

For me, this is the most beautiful spot in all of Indiana. Except in the fall, when the sightseers are taking in the colors, the place is very quiet. Few cars pass by on Hwy 62. For my money southern Indiana has the remainder of the state beat hands down when it comes to natural beauty. From Bloom-ington south to the Ohio River the land rises and falls in deep valleys and gorges. Forests pervade the countryside. From Bloomington north, especially north of Indianapolis, the land falls flat. In southern Indiana the earth is ruddy clay, not the black dirt of fertile central and northern Indiana. Limestone, sandstone, and coal are plentiful in southern Indiana. Southern Indiana is not so populous as the northern two-thirds of the state, and Evansville is the only city of size in the region.

Since southern Indiana lies in the Ohio River valley, the summers there suffer from the three H's: haze, heat, and humidity. The heat and the humidity get trapped down in that river valley creating this haze. It just sits there all fat and sassy until a thunderstorm blows it out. Then it starts all over again. Ugh!

So on this Sunday morning of July 24, 2016, having left Gethsemani earlier that morning after the ten-thirty Mass, I pull out of the parking lot of the Overlook Restaurant and make my final push for Saint Meinrad. Since the Abbey of Gethsemani is on Eastern Time and Saint Meinrad is on Central Time, I gain an hour on this two-hour drive heading west.

From Leavenworth to Saint Meinrad, Hwy 62 twists and turns and dips and climbs through some deep forest. You pass through the towns of Beechwood, Sulphur, West Fork, and St. Croix. I like St. Croix. For one thing, I like that name. In a region with towns called Sulphur, Eckerty, and Gnaw Bone, the name St. Croix is a delight for the tongue. For another thing, Holy Cross Church is there. Right along the highway. I've stopped there many times to pray the office before blowing into Saint Meinrad. The parish consists of around sixty-three families, seats about a hundred and fifty, and has one Sunday Mass at eight o'clock. The building is stone in the Romanesque style, complete with a single Byzantine tower. It's the architectural marvel of the area.

But I'm not stopping there today, although I give it a wave as I cruise by. I really want to get to the monastery.

I haven't been to Saint Meinrad in two years. I love the place. I have been going there since I was a kid. Mom liked to go for "a Sunday drive," so Dad would pack us all into the 1960 Chevy Impala, and off we'd go. Mom was not fussy about where we went for her Sunday drive, just so long as she *got out of the house.* Saint Meinrad was often the place.

We would stop at the Overlook in Leavenworth, where Mom and Dad would have a cup of coffee and smoke a couple of cigarettes. Mom always wanted a seat by the windows overlooking the river. Usually we got one, but when we didn't she would invariably say, "Well, maybe next time." Pile back into the car, and with Mom and Dad both smoking cigarettes up front, another twenty-eight miles to the monastery. Since no one in the car was Catholic, the monastery did not tug at the heartstrings of Roman devotion, and since no one in the car particularly cared about religion, the huge stone edifice to God on the Hill bore no sentimental wonder and awe. Rather, Dad liked the way the whole campus *looked.* To him the monastery looked like a castle. He liked the lakes that dotted the property. The grounds were well groomed. And all those people walking around in odd black "dresses" intrigued us all, with the inevitable question, "how can they stand being dressed like that in this *heat*?" always spewing forth with a shake of the head (remember, in the early to mid-1960s air-conditioning was not as ubiquitous as now).

You know you're almost to the monastery (if you're approaching it from the east), when you see the little brown sign announcing the turnoff for the Monte Cassino shrine (just five hundred feet away). More about the shrine later, though. As you pass that little sign, the monastery wings into view. It sits atop a hill. (The monks there frequently refer to the monastery as "the Hill," as in "Well, I've got to get back to the Hill.") The gold-colored crosses atop the twin spires glisten in the sun. It's an inspiring view.

At the western edge of the little town of Saint Meinrad, you hang a left. You drive up a little hill, fading right and then swinging left, and you turn into the parking lot of the guesthouse.

It's good to be back. I won't leave here until Friday, July 29. I'm looking forward to every minute of that time.

The reason I'm here is to attend a conference on Gregorian Chant. It's officially titled "Bringing to Life the Word of God in Song: Studies in the Form and Analysis of Gregorian Chant," and the conference is being given by Fr. Columba Kelly, OSB, of Saint Meinrad Archabbey. Fr. Kelly is to Gregorian Chant scholarship what Michael Jordan is to basketball: world-renowned, unparalleled, and groundbreaking. Close to thirty people from around the United States and Canada are attending this conference. Two books are required: *Gregorian Chant: A Guide to the History and Liturgy* by Daniel Saulnier, and the *Graduale Triplex*. We will meet from Monday through Friday, 9:00 a.m. to 11:00 a.m. and 2:00 p.m. to 4:00 p.m. each day. Each day, that is, except Tuesday. We will not meet at all on Tuesday morning.

I gather my gear from the trunk of my car and lug it to the front desk of the guesthouse. I tell the woman behind the desk who I am and why I'm here. She hands me an envelope that contains two key cards.

"You're in Gregory Hall 307," she tells me. "Do you know where that is?"

I do indeed. It's located right next to the church. The rooms in the guesthouse are very nice, and I love staying in them, but you have to walk the distance of a football field from the guesthouse in order to get to the archabbey church, whereas being housed in Gregory Hall, even though I still have to go outside to get to the church, I have to make only a few steps, and even then that area is within a roofed arcade. Very monastic!

Once I make it to Gregory Hall I take the elevator up to the third floor. The elevator dumps me out in a little vestibule, and then I turn right and walk nearly to the end of the third-floor hallway. Room 307 is on my right, three rooms from the end of the hall. I slide the key card into the slot, the little green light flickers, and I'm in my home away from home for the next several days.

I am immediately smitten with the room. At least fourteen-foot ceilings. Spacious bathroom, including a shower in which you can actually turn without bumping into the shower walls, and a toilet that—when flushed—would make a bowling ball disappear in an instant and with no trouble. A firm mattress. A bedstand. A desk with a hutch and a convenient light. A bookshelf. A chest of drawers. An armoire. A very comfortable rocking chair. And the air conditioner set so low you could hang beef in the room.

They know how to make you comfortable at Saint Meinrad.

However, the *pièce de resistance* is just outside my two arched windows: the archabbey church looms large and formidable, and—I love this—I can clearly hear the bells of the church that ring every quarter hour . . . all through the night! Is this going to be great or what?!

It is only one thirty, and since the conference doesn't start until tomorrow, Monday, I'm free the rest of the day to relax. So after putting all my stuff in order and plugging in my lap-top, I kick off my shoes and lie down for a nap.

Sleep, however, won't come. I'm too excited about being here. So I just lie there and listen to the church bells chime at fifteen-minute intervals. As my body relaxes my mind begins to wander. Mostly I think about the retreats I had here with my younger son John.

John and I first came here together in 2003. This was before the current guesthouse was built. This older guesthouse was a cinderblock structure built, I think, in the 1950s. We stayed in room E4 that first year. John was twelve. Before coming to Saint Meinrad for retreats, John and I would go to Saint Procopius in Lisle, Illinois.

Saint Meinrad, though, afforded us so much more acreage in which to walk. We would walk down to the Abbey Gift Shop and to the Scholar Shop. We would stroll over to the lakes, usually walking through the cemetery where the monks were buried. He and I both marveled at the dates on the headstones, such as 1881, 1870, 1900, etc.

At all of these retreats, either at Saint Meinrad or Saint Procopius, we would only stay two nights. That was enough. One year John and I were at Saint Meinrad on July 4. Not many people can say they saw fireworks at a monastery.

Ding-DONG. Ding-DONG. It is the bottom of the hour. The bells ease me from rumination and back to the moment. I rise from the comfortable bed and slip on my sandals. The red numerals of the clock on the bedstand read two thirty. Time for None.

I grab volume 3 of the *Liturgy of the Hours* that I had placed on the bedstand and head outside.

Saint Meinrad prays neither Terce nor None, at least not together in the archabbey church. The community does come together to pray Sext, but they refer to that Hour as Midday Prayer. So whenever I'm at Saint Meinrad on retreat I pray Terce and None by strolling along the concrete walkway that runs in front of the monastery buildings.

Of course, since this is late July, the air is hot, humid, and uncomfortable. When I step out into the air my glasses immediately steam up. Ugh!

If I'm praying the Hours on my own, as I'm doing now, I pray the Complementary Psalms at the Little Hours; that is, Psalms 120–22 at Terce, Psalms 123–25 at Sext, Psalms 126–28 at None. I like those psalms. They are short and easy to memorize.

The reading for None on Sunday in the Seventeenth Week of Ordinary time is from Galatians. As I walk down the walkway I come to the conclusion of the reading: "let us do good to all men—but especially those of the household of the faith."

The household of the faith. That phrase strikes me, and I take a seat on one of the red wooden benches that line the walkway to ponder it. In regard to the monks, I ask myself, would *the household of the faith* be *specifically* the community of monks? The western face of the archabbey church is right in front of me. The afternoon sun is splashing onto the ancient sandstone, and the crosses atop the spires glisten—twinkle, nearly. I know the monks pray for all Christians, but the monastic community at Saint Meinrad would have to be—for them—the "household of the faith." Right?

I conclude the Hour and head for the archabbey church. I approach not the doors on the west end of the church but the door on the north part of the church. The air-conditioned church feels good as I enter. Once inside I immediately turn left, because I want to go to the east end of the church, in the apse, and pray before the Blessed Sacrament.

I pass behind the north choir stalls, and just as I am about to enter the apse, the door on my left, the door that leads to the living quarters of the monks, catches my eye. One of the two doors is open, and I can see down the long hallway that leads to the living quarters (construction in that area is just being wrapped up). But on the other door, the door that is closed, is the sign:

> *Monastic Enclosure*
> *Private Area*

The household of the faith.

I love the way Saint Meinrad prays the Liturgy of the Hours. First of all, when you walk into the archabbey church a monk is standing there to greet you and to hand you the worship aid for that particular Hour. Second, unlike at New Melleray or Gethsemani, the guests at Saint Meinrad are not physically separated from the monks. New Melleray and Gethsemani both have an iron gate that demarcates the guest area from the monks. Saint Meinrad has no such demarcation. The chairs where the guests sit are right next to the choir stalls. I like that. Makes me feel like I'm part of the team instead of a spectator.

Another thing I love about Saint Meinrad: the bells peal for fifteen minutes before the beginning of Vigils and Vespers. *And* the bells are pealed by a monk (I'm guessing a novice) pulling on ropes. Very nice!

This hour is Vespers. I accept the worship aid from the monk standing at the door and take a seat in the front row of chairs. Since this is Sunday Second Vespers, the monks process in (as opposed to simply coming into choir as each monk enters the church individually). Walking in pairs, they begin behind the south choir, process west and around the Black Madonna that stands in the southwest corner of the church, continue to the baptismal font in the middle of the west end of the church, proceed walking east and bowing to the altar when they approach it (the altar is at the western end of the archabbey church), and finish by processing east down the middle of the church and into their choir stalls. However, before stepping into the stalls, the two monks who processed together turn to face one another, bow, then do an about-face and proceed up into the stalls. In this procession the novices and juniors lead the procession, with the seniors following. The abbot sits in the north choir, the first stall to the west of the break.

The psalms of Vespers are sung without an antiphon. Furthermore, the psalms go back and forth between a lone cantor and the remainder of the choir, as opposed to one side of the choir singing a stanza and the other side singing a stanza. In all my years of coming to Saint Meinrad, I have never heard a poor cantor. Always spot on.

I thought the first meeting of the conference was at nine o'clock Monday morning July 25, but not so. The first conference is not until two o'clock that afternoon.

I decide to do a little exploring.

My first adventure is the Monte Cassino shrine. The shrine is a mile away and up a steep hill. In cooler weather I could walk it, but with the Big Heat and Mr. Humidity coming along as well, there's no way I can go there on foot. I'll drive it, thank you very much!

I walk from Gregory Hall, over to the guesthouse, *through* the guesthouse, out into the parking lot of the guesthouse, and to my car. The inside of the car is already an oven, and it's only about ten after nine in the morning.

I drive back down off the hill and turn east on Hwy 62. A mile away on the twisting road is the turnoff to the shrine. I hang a left and start the steep climb up the twisting road. The climb is not a long one, though, and I quickly gain the crest of the hill.

And there it is, about a football field away, down on the right. It's a small, simple sandstone structure dedicated in 1871. Inside are about twelve or so creaky wooden pews. An altar is at the east end of the shrine, and Mass is celebrated there on Saturdays by one of the monks from the monastery. Public pilgrimages are held each Sunday in May and October. Rosary, procession, the whole nine yards. Draws a crowd too.

It's very quiet. No other vehicle in sight save a pickup truck parked by the shrine. As I approach the shrine, I notice that a deep ditch has been dug around the entire perimeter. Orange plastic fencing surrounds the whole work site. Buttressing the foundation, perhaps? I glide slowly by in my car, and as I reach the north side of the shrine, I see two bare-chested men brandishing digging tools. The older man pushes a shovel, while the younger man swings an ax. The two men are standing in the ditch that comes up to their waists. They stop and turn to take a look at who is driving by. They wave. I wave back. I won't be able to enter the shrine this trip.

So I drive back down the hill and toward the monastery. But instead of driving to the monastery, I swing left onto Hwy 545 and drive a half mile or so down the road to the Abbey Gift Shop. This shop sits at the bottom of the hill of the monastery, just to the south and east.

The shop carries the usual Catholic bric-a-brac: statues, crucifixes, icons, books, CDs, prayer cards, sympathy cards, even caskets (the monastery is in the casket business). I'm not in search of any of that. I'm hunting for a new Saint Meinrad ball cap. The beige one I'm wearing has seen better days. In fact, the tip of the bill of the hat is held together by Scotch tape. I once inadvertently drove over it with my car (long story). My wife threatens to toss it when I'm not looking (I suspect she secretly wants to burn it).

Sure enough, I locate a ball cap, but it comes bundled with a Saint Meinrad gray T-shirt. Twenty-something dollars. I buy it. Cash!

Some men collect coins or beer cans. Others dabble in model trains or yo-yos. I go to monasteries. So what's with the cap and shirt? Gotta show the colors, man.

By coincidence a friend of mine is at Saint Meinrad the same time I'm here. His name is Hal Jopp. He is a deacon from the diocese of Wilmington, Delaware. Hal is at Saint Meinrad for the week with his "deacon guys."

Hal is the director of diaconate formation for his diocese, and Saint Meinrad is the institution that provides the instructors for all the courses the men have to take. The program takes four years, and the men meet once a month for an entire weekend from September through June for the duration of the four years. However, in the summer before the final year, the men travel to Saint Meinrad for a weeklong course in homiletics. That is why Hal is at Saint Meinrad; he's here with the eight men who are taking the homiletics course.

Hal and I met when one year we just happened to be in the Monastic Center at New Melleray at the same time. Since he lives in Maryland and I live in Illinois, the only time we meet is when we're at New Melleray . . . or here at Saint Meinrad.

Hal and one of the other deacon wannabes flew into Louisville for this one-week course, then rented a car and drove the eighty-odd miles to Saint Meinrad. In an earlier e-mail to Hal I had advised him that on his drive to Saint Meinrad from Louisville, he should stop at the Overlook in Leavenworth. I told him if he were lucky he'd see a barge or two try to negotiate that horseshoe bend in the river. When I met up with Hal at Saint Meinrad, one of the first things he said to me was "You were right. We saw a barge at that bend."

At 1:50 p.m. on that same day I leave room 307 and head down to the first floor of Gregory Hall. I'm looking for room 160. That's where the chant conference is to be held.

About five people are already present when I stroll in. Fr. Kelly is not yet there. In the next ten minutes, though, the room fills up nicely, until about thirty of us are present. Fr. Kelly walks into the room at two o'clock on the nose.

We're lucky he's both in the classroom as well as still alive. About three weeks before our conference, the eighty-five-year-old Kelly was driving up to St. Joseph College in Rensselaer, Indiana, to give a conference. Once off I-65, he was driving down a state highway that was under road construction. Somehow Fr. Kelly lost control of his vehicle, went off the road, and rolled the vehicle.

But he is here with us this day. We see no visible bruises. He remains seated the whole time he teaches.

He introduces the class and holds up the two required texts to make sure we have them, and George Hubbard, staff organist at the monastery, hands out a forty-page photocopy titled "Handout notes for Chant Class."

We're about thirty minutes into this class when it becomes obvious to me that I'm in way over my head. Kelly is using vocabulary that is beyond me: *neume*, *punctum*, *clivis*, *salicus*, and *Laon*. He uses phrases I've heard but don't understand: *minor thirds*, *triads*, *pretonic syllables*. I learn very quickly that my classmates are either (1) directors of music at their parishes or (2) professors of music at a college.

I'm neither. True, I have an acceptable singing voice, and I can sing on key. But I can't read music, and I have to learn a piece of music (such as the *Exsultet*) by ear, listening to it over and over again until I have it memorized. That's about it.

But I'm fascinated by the class. We sing, and as we do, Kelly swings his arms and cries, "Think of a child on a swing! Chant should flow like you're on a swing!" When we stop, he has us swing our own arms while we repeat the chant.

He throws in all kinds of historical asides that put chant in historical context. For example, the long chants at that part of the Mass where the gifts are brought forward. "It used to be that the bishop and the deacon would have to go some distance to receive the bread and wine," Kelly explained. "To fill that time the choir would sing these long chants."

Fr. Kelly has a good sense of humor and knows how to tell a good story. So despite my musical ignorance I stayed on. I learned a lot, and it was fun, especially when we all sang together.

One of the first chants we go over is the *Sanctus* from Mass. The heading over the piece reads "Sanctus XVIII," so I suppose that means something. Anyway, he has us chant it. Well, we're too wooden in doing so. "Too choppy," Fr. Kelly tells us. "Remember the swing," and he swings his arm back and forth. "Try it again, and swing your arm like this," and he demonstrates. We try again. He stops us. "Read the text," says Fr. Kelly. "Just read it." We do. "Notice you had inflection in your voice," he says. "You didn't pronounce each word with the same emphasis. Same goes in chant. It flows." We crank up the *Sanctus* again, and this time we sing it all the way through. "There!" Fr. Kelly cries, "You got it."

Later that night I finally begin to catch on to what Fr. Kelly is trying to teach us.

Right after Compline on Monday night Br. Maurus, the guestmaster at Saint Meinrad, hauls out into the middle of the vestibule of the guesthouse a cart filled with wine, cheese, crackers, chips, nuts, and other assorted snacks. He also drags in two large coolers iced down with water, soft drinks, and beer.

Didn't I say that Saint Meinrad knows how to take care of you?

After a while, the group breaks up into smaller groups. We're drinking wine and beer, and finally I confess to the group I'm in that for the most part I don't know what the hell is going on in the class. That comment, plus the beer and wine, really breaks the ice. One guy goes to his room and returns with his copy of the *Graduale Triplex*, and he and the others begin filling me in on vocabulary and other things. He sits down next to me with the *Triplex* open and begins to show me what all those squiggly lines that are above and below the staff mean. The five of us stay there in the vestibule until close at ten o'clock. Our conversation about the class and other church matters is great. I learn quite a bit from them. It's in such little groups as these that conferences really hit their stride and are worthwhile.

But I'm running out of gas, so I bid them all a good night. I want to be fresh for tomorrow's big festivity: the abbatial blessing of Abbot Kurt Stasiak.

Abbot Kurt was elected abbot back on June 2. It is just pure coincidence that the abbatial blessing occurs at the same time as the chant conference. I'm excited about participating in this Mass. What are the odds that I'll ever participate in another one?

Tuesday, July 26, dawns foggy. The weather forecast says a 60 percent chance of thunderstorms. However, when the morning fog burns off, the sky is clear enough. Of course, it's humid, just 96 percent. Need gills to breathe!

Six flagpoles are planted at the base of the steps at the western end of the archabbey church: three Vatican City flags and three flags bearing the coat of arms of Saint Meinrad Archabbey.

The Mass is set to start at ten o'clock. Yesterday, before Fr. Kelly dismissed the class, he advised us to get in the church no later than nine thirty. Hal and I park ourselves in chairs near the altar at nine fifteen. Good thing, too, the place fills up fast.

The procession begins at ten with a fanfare from the organ. The procession takes a little over seven minutes. First in the procession are the monks of Saint Meinrad, both brothers and priests. Processing in with the Saint Meinrad monks is a Cistercian monk from, I'm guessing, nearby Gethsemani. Hal and I look at one another with a nod upon noticing the Trappist presence. Next, the visiting priests file in. They are seated in chairs at the far western end of the archabbey church, west of the altar. Abbots (I believe nine) from other monasteries process in next. The abbots are wearing white miters. I recognize four of the abbots: Abbot Urban Federer from Saint Meinrad's motherhouse, Einsiedeln Abbey in Switzerland; Abbot Elias Dietz from Gethsemani; Abbot Austin Murphy from Saint Procopius Abbey in Lisle, Illinois; and Abbot Vincent Bataille of Marmion Abbey in Aurora, Illinois. Abbot Vincent is the current president of the Swiss-American Congregation to which Saint Meinrad belongs. Also, Abbot Vincent has been in my classroom. A colleague of mine (Jeff Ptacek) and I invited Abbot Vincent to come speak to our classes about monasticism.

Just to put things into perspective: Archabbot Kurt is the tenth abbot of Saint Meinrad; Abbot Urban is the fifty-ninth abbot of Einsiedeln.

The procession continues with a couple of bishops, and bringing up the rear is Abbot Kurt, followed by the archbishop of Indianapolis and the presider of the Mass, Joseph Tobin, CSsR (Congregation of the Most Holy Redeemer). The abbots and bishops sit in the choir stalls with the monks. Abbot Kurt is seated next to the archbishop. With all in place, the Mass continues as usual.

After Archbishop Tobin's homily, which I think is quite strong, comes all of the fun stuff: Abbot Kurt lying prostrate while the Litany of the Saints is chanted, Archbishop Tobin bestowing on Abbot Kurt the miter and crosier, and the special address given to Abbot Kurt by Archbishop Tobin while he is seated in a chair in front of the archbishop.

The whole Mass moves smoothly. I detect no gaffes, blunders, or absurd notions. Furthermore, it moves surprisingly quickly: the men start processing out of the archabbey church at the one hour and fifty-five-minute mark. And because of either excitement or hunger, the procession out is two minutes shorter than the procession in. It's now noon; time to eat!

Hal and I beat a hasty retreat out of the archabbey church; about four hundred hungry people are descending on the dining room in Newman Hall. We don't want to be stuck way back in line!

When Hal and I arrive in Newman, with about ten folks in front of us, the monks are already there waiting to serve us. Many of them are wearing aprons, and they are waving us up to the serve-yourself food line. All the tables in the dining room are dressed with white tablecloths. A vase of flowers is on each table. Carafes of water and tea sit atop the tables, as do bottles of merlot. The menu? Meat loaf (thickly sliced), mashed potatoes, steamed vegetables, and a garden salad. When the wine runs out, and it does, the monks bring another bottle to the table.

Can you say hospitality?

I sit with Hal, a few of his deacon guys, and Dr. Richard Stern, professor of homiletics at the seminary run by Saint Meinrad, who is teaching the course on homiletics to Hal's deacon guys. Nice conversation. Everyone is impressed by the liturgy.

When I go back up to the food line to fetch some dessert, I run into Abbot Vincent. "I'm back in the classroom this upcoming year," he tells me. I just assume he means the classroom at the University of St. Mary of the Lake Seminary in Mundelein, Illinois, where he had been on staff. "No," he tells me when I mention the seminary, "at Marmion Academy. I'm going to be teaching seniors."

Marmion Academy is a college prep high school run by the monks at Marmion Abbey. It is an all-boys school. "Seniors are a killer in that second semester," I tell him. "Yeah, I've taught 'em before," he tells me.

After eating I return to the archabbey church to pray Sext. No one is there, and it is nice being in the church after all the fuss and bother of the earlier abbatial blessing. I stroll around the perimeter of the church praying the Hour.

The day is Tuesday around one in the afternoon. The rest of the world is hard at their jobs, scratching out a living for themselves and their families. Yet, here I am in this beautiful archabbey church praying psalms after having eaten a wonderful lunch and having witnessed an abbatial blessing.

I have to be the luckiest man in the world.

The next morning, Wednesday, I'm walking out of room 307 just moments before the bells begin to peal for Vigils and Lauds. I like to hit that little arcade just as the bells begin to peal at five fifteen. I had set the alarm for five o'clock, but as usual at this stage in my life, I don't need an alarm. I just wake up well before I have to.

Sure enough, I'm not two steps out the door of Gregory Hall down on the ground floor when the bells begin to peal. "Time to pray, boys!" the bells seem to be saying.

Vigils at Saint Meinrad is very soothing. The psalms are recited—slowly and softly—back and forth between the two choirs (the psalms are recited in a similar way at Midday Prayer). No antiphons. When it is time to start a psalm one of the monks stands, recites the first line of the psalm, then sits back down as the choir on his side recites the remainder of the stanza. Then the other choir recites.

During the week I'm at Saint Meinrad, a monk in the north choir introduces the psalm. He sits in the second row, first stall west of the break. He has a good voice, strong, but not overpowering. Very good diction and cadence; he obviously knows how a sentence flows. The same monk also proclaims the readings both at office and in Mass. It's a pleasure listening to him.

I notice one thing that intrigues me: before this monk stands and proclaims the first line of the psalm, I notice he is looking intently across the way at the south choir. He is looking, not in some meditative manner off into space, but as if he is watching a single person over in that south choir. Waiting for a signal, perhaps, to stand and recite? If so, from whom?

Up for today at the chant conference? Saint Meinrad psalm modes. Now that is something I can understand!

There are eight psalm modes, all composed by Fr. Kelly. The modes can be chanted to either four- or six-line stanzas. I am familiar with two modes. I frequently sing them when I pray office. However, I cannot identify the mode by just hearing it. In other words, I cannot either sing the mode or hear it sung and say, "Hey, that's Mode N." Of course, the solution is to play the tones on a piano and get to know them that way. I do not have a piano, and I do not read music, so that idea doesn't work.

Fr. Kelly dives right into the modes when class begins, a respite from the *Graduale Triplex*! We simply start singing a four-line stanza of eight different psalms, a different mode per psalm. It's fun, and, of course, the class—filled with real musicians—picks up on the tones very quickly.

Turns out that the two modes I know are Mode 3 and Mode 7.

Then Fr. Kelly drops a bit of information I find fascinating. "Most of the monks in the choir have no clue what mode they are singing," Kelly says. "The books they're looking at in choir don't announce the mode. They just have them memorized. Except for maybe the novices." That really got my attention. I just assumed that the monks in choir could be told, "Hey, let's chant this in Mode 7," and wham! they would be right on it.

"It doesn't matter whether or not they can identify the specific mode," Kelly continued. "What matters is that the tone is a part of them, and when they hear it introduced by the cantor, they know exactly how to sing it. When the mode is an integral part of your being, then it is true prayer."

Obviously, then, the cantor must know the individual modes. "The cantor will know," Kelly said.

The class today is livelier, almost childlike, in fact. I think it's because we're singing pieces that are in English and in a far simpler melody. Fr. Kelly runs through the modes quickly and wants to move back to the *Triplex*, but several in the class ask if we can sing another mode, and so we do.

In the second half of class this morning we return to the *Graduale Triplex*; we tackle the *Comedite pinguia*. However, this time Fr. Kelley starts us off by singing a simpler version of it by having us sing just the "foundation" tones. This version appears in the notes he passed out to us. We run through that three times, and then we return to the full version as given in the *Triplex*. Yep, it was easier learning it that way.

Before Vespers that evening I walk over to the guesthouse; I want to look through the small library over there. The library is located on the first floor of the guesthouse at the far end of the hall.

The whole guesthouse is quiet. I neither see nor hear anyone as I walk down the hall. The library is empty. I scan some titles and select *Monastic Practices* by Charles Cummings, OCSO. I take it to the table and sit down. The window looks out on the driveway that runs adjacent to the guesthouse.

I open the book. It's a good one; I've read it before. I can't, however, concentrate. So I just flip through the pages, stopping now and then to scan a sentence or a paragraph. I come across this:

> The customs in a monastery all have their part in the total
> process of transformation taking place in monastic life. They
> invite us to surrender to them, to trust them, to listen for
> their inmost meaning, to grow with them and be nourished
> by them for a lifetime. No single one of these customs may

be essential to monastic life, but taken together and lived with generosity they help constitute an environment that opens one to the encounter with God.[1]

I feel a sense of loneliness, and that puzzles me, for I cannot account for it. I try to imagine what it must be like to be a monk here or at Gethsemani or New Melleray and try to learn all the customs that belong to the respective houses. How long does it take to learn them? What is the level of precedence for each of them? Are you punished if you fail to observe them? What is the punishment? I soon surrender such rumination. There is no way I can possibly know, so why bother?

Then I think to myself: Do you think monks gather together sometimes and ask themselves, "How do married people know they're marrying the right one? What are the priorities in raising children? What do you do if one of them loses a job?"

One group gazes out upon the other and tries to comprehend the other, and all the while I imagine God is just shaking his head.

Tomorrow, Thursday, is my last full day here.

Hal and I sit together at Vespers on Thursday evening. It's a ferial day, so the monks do not process in as they did on Sunday evening but simply file into their stalls individually. Hal and I are sitting alongside of the south choir, and from our vantage point neither one of us can see the cantor, who is in a stall farther east.

Vespers cranks up. The opening verse (*O God, come to my assistance*) and hymn are chanted. Now the psalmody. No antiphon, just the cantor intoning the first line of the psalm in one of the modes (which one!?). The cantor seems a little shaky on it, but he recovers well. The choir falls right into the tone on

---

[1] Charles Cummings, *Monastic Practices*, rev. ed., MW 75 (Collegeville, MN: Cistercian Publications, 2015), 63–64.

the next line with no problem. At the conclusion of the psalm is the Glory Be.

Next psalm. Again the cantor intones it. This time, however, he is way off pitch. It is obvious to both Hal and me; we look at one another with facial expressions that say, "What was that?" In the mere seconds it takes to chant the first line, I'm wondering if the choir will be able to respond on pitch. It does, though, and off we go chanting that psalm just fine, thank you very much!

The final psalm and the responsory, also intoned by the cantor, go well.

So I was very surprised when, at the conclusion of Vespers, I saw what I saw.

At the conclusion of every Hour in choir, the monks don't just file out willy-nilly. Rather they file out in order of seniority. The abbot files out first, descending from his back stall, then the other senior monks file out, also descending from the back row of stalls, then the middle row of stalls, and finally the younger monks and novices filing out last. Well, at the conclusion of Vespers this evening, the abbot descends out of the choir as normal from the north choir. Coming out of the south choir is another monk, not a senior monk from the back row of stalls in the south choir. This monk and the abbot turn and face the altar that is at the western end of the archabbey church. The abbot then spins around and departs, and the other monk . . . kneels down on the Italian marble floor. He remains kneeling there until all the other monks—seniors and novices—have filed out of the choir stalls. He then stands, bows to the altar, and walks away.

He was the cantor. He was doing penance for his mistake in choir.

Thursday evening I pack up as much as I can and drag it out to the car. I check out at the desk in the guesthouse early that evening, for I'll be leaving the next day before anyone is at the desk.

The next morning, Friday, July 29, I attend Vigils and Lauds and eat a light breakfast with Hal and a few of his deacon guys over in Newman. Just some orange juice and a cinnamon roll. I wolf it down and then bid adieu to all.

"I'll be at New Melleray in early June," I tell Hal.

"Margaret and I are going up to Alaska twice this fall to visit our son," Hal says. "We'll see about New Melleray."

"E-mail you about it in January?" I ask.

"That'll be good."

We shake hands and I leave.

I have just a tad over four hundred miles of driving ahead of me. You know the old saying: there are really just two seasons—winter and road construction. I have something to look forward to.

I have really enjoyed this whole week being at both Gethsemani and Saint Meinrad.

I don't use a GPS to tell me where to go; I navigate by Mr. Rand McNally. I consult the atlas and determine my route. East on I-64 to State Highway 37. North through Paoli, Orleans, Mitchell, and Bedford. Continue north on Hwy 37 around Bloomington (Go IU!) and on up to the southern edge of Indianapolis, where I'll pick up I-465. West and north on I-465, and pick up I-65 on the northern end of Indianapolis. I-65 to Gary, where I'll merge onto I-80/94. Around Chicago on the Tri-State (I-294) and exit on its far northern end at Illinois Hwy 120. West on it through Grayslake, right past our parish, St. Gilbert, and on into Fox Lake.

I won't listen to anything in the car on the nearly eight-hour drive home (I plan on stopping at Bloomington to eat). Why? After all that prayer and silence at the monastery, after all that chant, after all the reflection, the car radio or music is like fingernails on a blackboard. It takes me awhile to ease back into the world.

One last Saint Meinrad story. Back in late April 2009 when I was director of diaconate formation for the Diocese of Gary, the handful of men who would be ordained deacons in June of that year and I were down at Saint Meinrad. The occasion was the five-day canonical retreat required of the men to be ordained. Also with us was Ted Mauch, a seminarian from the Diocese of Gary who was attending Sacred Heart Seminary in Detroit. Ted would be ordained deacon in June along with my handful of guys; however, Ted was studying for the priesthood and would subsequently be ordained priest in June 2010. I have known Ted since he was a student in my eighth-grade religious education class at St. Joseph Church in La Porte, Indiana. Even as an eighth grader Ted wanted to be a priest.

So we are all down there at Saint Meinrad. On Wednesday evening, April 29, all of us are at the UnStable, a student-operated pub on campus (Saint Meinrad operates a seminary and school of theology). It's a good place to relax with friends while chowing down on beer and pizza. The several televisions scattered here and there on the walls are usually tuned to sports.

So we're knocking back the beer and pizza that night when in walk eight young women. I peg them all to be in their early twenties. One of these young women caught the eyes of every man in the UnStable. This raven-haired lass was drop-dead gorgeous. Probably about five-foot-five. Full lips painted red. She was wearing a turquoise halter top, and she filled it out so well that Russ Meyer (of "Faster, Pussycat! Kill! Kill!" fame) would have been proud. What do these young women proceed to do? Shoot pool. Let me tell you, when the raven-haired lass leaned over to line up her shot? No one was watching television at that moment.

So I leaned back to catch Ted's attention. He was sitting several men down from me. "Hey, Ted," I had to nearly shout because of all the noise. "Do young damsels like her ever grace the corridors of Sacred Heart Seminary up in Detroit?"

"Never," Ted shouted back. "Young women never darken the corners of Sacred Heart Seminary except for special occasions like ordinations."

You just never know who is going to walk into a monastery.

There are other monasteries, of course. The three I visit just happen to be in the region where I live. A few summers ago my wife Sara and I visited Saint John's Abbey up in College- ville, Minnesota. I really liked it there. She and I prayed Mid- day Prayer right there in the choir with the monks. Loved it! Sara, though, was very self-conscious about being the only woman in the whole choir. I bought this cool T-shirt. It's black. In white letters, in a medieval-looking script, is the first word of the Rule: *Listen*. Above that word, in light blue lettering—but not in a medieval script—is the line "Listen carefully, my son, to the master's instructions." Below the word *listen* in white lettering is the phrase, again in light blue, "and attend to them with the ear of your heart." On the right sleeve is a white cross with the words *St. John's Abbey*, also in white lettering.

Gotta show the colors, man.

The three monasteries I visit on a somewhat regular basis have different personalities. New Melleray and Gethsemani are Cistercian or Trappist;[2] Saint Meinrad is Benedictine. I would say New Melleray is delightful; Gethsemani, serious; and Saint Meinrad, fun.

Which monastery you visit (distance and costs aside) should be determined by what is going on in your life at that moment, whether or not you have ever visited a monastery before, and the length of time you want to stay.

I feel blessed to have these three monasteries within a rea- sonable driving distance. But I want to add two more soon to my repertoire: Marmion Abbey in Aurora, Illinois, and Saint John's up in Collegeville.

---

[2] Monastic descendants of the New Monastery founded at Cîteaux in 1198 are known as Cistercians; those Cistercian communities descended from the seventeenth-century reform movement at La Trappe Abbey, officially the Cistercian Order of the Strict Observance (OCSO), are frequently also known as Trappists. Non-Trappist Cistercians are members of the Cistercian Order of the Common Observance (OCist). All follow the Rule of Saint Benedict, but the two Cistercian Orders are distinct from the Order of Saint Benedict (OSB) or Benedictines.

What says the psalmist?

> *How lovely is your dwelling place,*
> *Lord, God of hosts.*
> *My soul is long and yearning,*
> *is yearning for the courts of the Lord*
>
> *They are happy, who dwell in your house,*
> *forever singing your praise.* (Ps 83:2-3, 5)

That says it all.

PART TWO

Mimesis

Discern, Discern, Discern

Around 1750 there were in the whole of Catholic Europe at least 350,000 inmates of monasteries out of a total population of less than a hundred million, a proportion of rather more than 1 in 300. . . . In Spain and Italy nearly 1 person in 100 was a monk or nun.[1]

What happened?!

In the spring of 2007, twenty-two year old Jeff Ptacek sat in a nook tucked away inside St. Procopius Abbey, just down the hall from the abbey church. Jeff, having prayed Lauds and eaten breakfast with the monastic community, was collecting his thoughts. In a half hour he would walk twenty minutes down, through a wooded trail, to Benedictine University, a school operated by the Benedictine monks of St. Procopius. Jeff was a senior at the university, with majors in philosophy, history, and education. Classes loomed ahead for the day.

Jeff was content. He enjoyed living off and on at the monastery and attending classes at the university. He also enjoyed being with his girlfriend Sarah Solarz, whom he had dated since his junior year at East Leyden High School in Franklin Park, Illinois, a western suburb of Chicago. Sarah attended Benedictine University as well. She was an education major.

Living "off and on" at the monastery? Well, yes. Beginning in the second semester of his junior year, Jeff began living in

---

[1] Derek Beales, *Prosperity and Plunder: European Catholic Monasteries in the Age of Revolution, 1650–1815* (Cambridge: Cambridge University Press, 2003), 2.

the cloister at St. Procopius, discerning a vocation to the monastery. He would live two weeks there, and then live a week at home with his parents in nearby River Grove or at Kucera Hall on campus.

Jeff's room within the cloister was small but efficient: twin bed, wooden wardrobe, desk, shower, toilet, and sink. The shower was actually large enough to enable a 360-degree turn without knocking over the Head & Shoulders from the little ledge. The sand-colored carpet on the floor in the main section of the room dovetailed with the off-white color of the walls. When Jeff was living at the monastery he sat in choir with the monks at office and ate with them in refectory.

Jeff liked the monastic day: prayer, work, study, community. For Jeff the monastic day made perfect sense. The day was ordered. It was calming. The bell rang and you did this. Lauds was over; you did that.

Ironically, Jeff didn't even know that the monastery existed when he enrolled in the college. All he knew was that the university had a teaching program. At freshmen orientation, though, about a hundred or so incoming students were led across and down the road to St. Procopius Abbey. At the front entrance to the monastery Abbot Hugh was waiting for them. The abbot was in his habit. Right outside the front doors, in a small plaza, is an iron (I think) statue of St. Procopius. The iron statue portrays Procopius with his arms outstretched. When Jeff saw the abbot standing there in his habit and pectoral cross and with a beard, and when Jeff took a closer look at that statue, he was intrigued. When Abbot Hugh escorted the students into the abbey church, which was still fragrant with incense burned earlier that day, Jeff was hooked.

So there Jeff sat in a nook at a monastery in the middle of the week getting ready to head off to classes. Life was great. The monastery was great.

Then the abbot walked by.

Abbot Hugh Anderson had been the eighth abbot of St. Procopius Abbey. At the time Jeff was living there discerning his vocation, Abbot Dismas was the acting abbot. Hugh was abbot emeritus.

Abbot Hugh was sixty-four years old when Jeff was at St. Procopius. Tall and sporting a white short-cropped beard, Abbot Hugh was a grounded, down-to-earth guy. He was simple, not flashy. He had a good laugh, the type of laugh that made you want to laugh along with him. He was also, in Seinfeld-ese, a "close talker."

On this particular morning Abbot Hugh was walking by the nook where Jeff was camped getting ready for his day. Abbot Hugh was not looking for Jeff, but when he saw Jeff he stopped abruptly. When Abbot Hugh entered the nook Jeff stood. Abbot Hugh stepped right up into Jeff's face (hence *close talker*) and leaned toward Jeff just enough so that the abbot's silver pectoral cross dangled in midair from around his neck.

"I want you to stop what you're doing," the abbot said to Jeff. The abbot's voice was not gruff, but it wasn't gentle, either. Abbot Hugh wanted to make sure Jeff got the message loud and clear.

"I want you to think about what your life is," Abbot Hugh continued. "Whatever that is, it can't be about you. It has to be what the Lord wants. So go and think about that."

And with that the abbot spun around and disappeared.

To say that Jeff was shocked would be an understatement. Actually, Jeff was angry not so much at the abbot, but at God.

He bolted out of the nook and strode down the hall. He ducked into the small Blessed Sacrament Chapel and dropped to his knees on the cushioned kneeler. He took some deep breaths to calm himself.

"You can't do this to me!" Jeff cried to God. Then Jeff spewed some profanity God's way. Jeff was 100 percent sure that he was called to both the monastery and to Sarah.

Calm followed the profanity.

"So I cleared my head," said Jeff years later, "and tried to not think about anything. Some time passed." What would it be? Postulant or Sarah? "Then I told myself I would go with whatever popped into my mind first."

His first thought was Sarah.

We refer to it as "calling one's hand." That's exactly what Abbot Hugh did, called Jeff's hand. Discernment is fine, but discernment leads to a decision; discernment is good, but it is not the end.

Jeff wasn't ready to have his hand called, hence his being unsettled by it all.

"I was leaning toward the monastery," said Jeff. "I was coming to the end of my senior year, and I knew I had to make a decision."

Abbot Hugh's words were simply a wake-up call.

Abbot Hugh may have supplied the wake-up call, but it was Br. Guy who had stirred the pot. Two years before Abbot Hugh called Jeff's hand, Jeff met—at the recommendation of Abbot Hugh—with Br. Guy, who at the time was a minister on the campus of Benedictine University. Br. Guy was neither abbot nor priest, and he was closer in age to Jeff than was Abbot Hugh. In retrospect Jeff believes that Abbot Hugh wanted Jeff to meet a regular monk.

The two men met right after the midday meal in the office of campus ministry. Topic of conversation? Monastic life.

Jeff had been wowed by what he had seen already at the monastery. Br. Guy wanted Jeff to see more.

"There's no bullshit here," said Br. Guy. "There's going to be struggle with this life. The life is not easy. We think about women. That's part of our daily struggle."

Br. Guy knew of Jeff's girlfriend Sarah. "You're never going to get rid of her," said Br. Guy. "Trick is to learn how to live without her in this life."

As Jeff soaked it all in Br. Guy changed direction. "What do you want to do?" he asked Jeff. "How do you see your life as a monk?"

"I want to be a teacher," Jeff replied. Jeff thought that reasonable, what with the abbey running the university and all.

"Have you thought about the infirmary?" Br. Guy asked. "You might have to help take care of the old guys."

That held no appeal to Jeff at all. He was young, and he wanted to be in a profession with the young.

"Our meeting lasted less than an hour," Jeff later said. "I think Br. Guy was trying to help me not to romanticize monasticism." Jeff admits that at the time his view of monasticism was a romantic one. "I was attracted to the history of it," Jeff says now. "I saw myself as a monk playing a role in history."

But the monk's habit also caught Jeff's attention. "I was watching this monk one day. The wind was blowing, and he had his hood up. His scapular billowed out with the blowing of the wind. I loved that."

Jeff insists that Sarah never put any pressure on him. "If you're called to God, who am I to question that?" Jeff recalls Sarah telling him.

Rather, the pressure not to enter the monastery came from Mom (registered nurse) and Dad (a police officer). And the unusual routine of living two weeks at the monastery and then a week at home or on campus only elicited from Jeff's mother, "What the hell are you doing?"

Well, since the 2006–2007 academic year Jeff has been teaching in the department of religious studies at Carmel Catholic High School in Mundelein, Illinois. He and Sarah have been married five years. They have two sons. Sarah teaches at a Catholic elementary school. Jeff is a grand knight in the Knights of Columbus. Every day he prays the Liturgy of the Hours and reads the Rule. He sometimes sports a black T-shirt that bears the phrase on its front, "Honor your Inner Monk." Saint Meinrad's offers it for sale.

Don't you see? The conversation hasn't been settled; it only continues in a different form and at a different venue.

❖   ❖   ❖

PLAISS: You've got an Inner Monk T-shirt from Saint Meinrad. I have a Listen T-shirt from Saint John's Abbey. Why do two grown men wear such things?

PTACEK: Wishful thinking? I wear it as a call to focus on a way of life.

PLAISS: So what's the difference between us wearing monk shirts and fans wearing Cubs, Sox, Bears, or Blackhawks shirts?

PTACEK: The jersey is different. The jersey is about *me*. It gives me some sort of identity. If the Cubs or Sox win or lose, that doesn't help me. The Inner Monk shirt, the Listen shirt, is about praying more. It's about telling people, "Hey, these guys exist."

PLAISS: Why not become an oblate?

PTACEK: Of Procopius?

PLAISS: Yeah.

PTACEK: I will. I want to finish grad school first.

PLAISS: What's the attraction?

PTACEK: I like the idea of being an oblate. I'd be making a commitment to a monastery, a specific place. It will give me a greater sense of monastic life. I'm married and have children, but I can still have a monastic experience. I like Procopius. I want to be part of it in some fashion. And that's different from joining a third order. If I became a member of the third order of the Franciscans, I would not be attached to Marytown;[2] I'd be a part of an order. An oblate is attached to a particular house. I like that. Stability.

PLAISS: What do you think of claustral oblates?

---

[2] Marytown is a community of the Order of Franciscan Minors Conventual (also known as the Conventual Franciscans), just down the street from Carmel Catholic High School.

PTACEK: I think there are men called to that. Obviously, I'm not one.

PLAISS: You don't think they're like "a little bit pregnant"? I mean, if you're living in the monastery as a monk, just be one, you know?

PTACEK: Could be circumstances that we don't know.

PLAISS: Why don't the monasteries attract as many people as before? I mean as full-fledged monks?

PTACEK: A radical sense of individualism. You're not going to tell me when I can go to bed. You're not going to tell me I can't use my phone. You're not going to tell me I can't leave here for a few hours. You can't tell me, you can't tell me, you can't tell me. . . .

PLAISS: Kardong notes in this book I read that one of the biggest obstacles to recruiting people to the monastery is the issue of privacy. People who approach the monastery as possible candidates have their own apartment or house, their own car, their own schedule, etc.

PTACEK: He's right.

PLAISS: Yeah, but when in the last seventy-five years has that not been the case?

PTACEK: Back in the day, the monastery was seen as a good life. The monastery would feed you, house you, educate you.

PLAISS: They still do that—some, anyway. The Benedictines. Education, I mean.

PTACEK: The radical sense of individualism.

PLAISS: So will they fold? The monasteries?

PTACEK: Some individual houses will. But I think the idea of monasticism will continue.

PLAISS: Blue Cloud in South Dakota is gone. Holy Trinity in Utah will be gone soon. Assumption down in Missouri is switching to the Cistercian Common Observance.

PTACEK: There you go.

PLAISS: The average age of many of the houses, especially the Trappists, is getting quite old.

PTACEK: That was one of *my* concerns at Procopius. Do I want to be the kid among all those old guys? Am I going to have to take care of them all alone? I think monasticism will evolve, not fold. Evolve into something we can't see yet. On the other hand, places like Saint Meinrad's, Saint John's, Saint Vincent's have guys numbering in the nineties or over a hundred, and they're getting young novices, too, multiple ones.

PLAISS: Yeah, when I was at New Melleray back in late May and early June I didn't see a postulant or novice. They have one junior. As you and I both know, monasticism is a tough sell to these kids.

PTACEK: It's the "you only live once" thing. They're not going to be strapped down. A monastery would be smothering to them. But it's not just religious life where this idea pops up. It's in all forms of life, and it's not just kids. Cohabitation instead of marriage. Try getting someone interested in the Knights. It's all over. People are afraid of commitment, because—

PLAISS: it's an infringement upon their freedom.

PTACEK: Right. But at the same time the kids are intrigued by monasticism.

PLAISS: Is that just because it's so foreign to them?

PTACEK: Maybe. But you know, in your spirituality class, the kids, many of them, like the Liturgy of the Hours. They're at least intrigued with it.

PLAISS: True. A few have approached me saying they like the "long" period of silence. All ten minutes of it. But I suppose that's ten minutes they don't get elsewhere.

PTACEK: So with your class and my Inner Monk stuff I give them, maybe out of a hundred and thirty students we'll touch two or three.

❖   ❖   ❖

I personally like what Thomas Merton wrote seventeen months before his death:

> The danger of education, I have found, is that it so easily confuses means with ends. Worse than that, it quite easily forgets both and devotes itself merely to the mass production of uneducated graduates—people literally unfit for anything except to take part in an elaborate and completely artificial charade that they and their contemporaries have conspired to call "life."[3]

I have mixed feelings about Merton's thoughts there, but I have read that pericope numerous times, and the phrase that keeps jumping out to me is "artificial charade."

Some people view monasticism as a charade. Some view the men and women who reside in monasteries as people who have deluded themselves. Now our age, our culture, is quick to add that if such people want to engage in such behavior, so be it. Frankly, such a lifestyle brings amused bafflement to many. Bernhard Eckerstorfer, a Benedictine monk in Austria, writes:

> In my abbey tour guides are asked again and again: "Are there still monks living here?" The word *still* reveals that monasticism is for many today a remnant of a past that seems distant and unreal, yet all the more fascinating. Whenever a group of tourists spots one of us in his habit, the monk

---

[3] Thomas Merton, *Selected Essays*, ed. Patrick F. O'Connell (Maryknoll, NY: Orbis Books, 2013), 439.

seems much more interesting than the best explanation of our 1,200 years of history.[4]

Fascinating, but harmless. For our age, our culture, monasticism is exactly what Christianity should be: off by itself and off the beaten path, affecting no one save those who choose to believe it—but let the rest of us thinking people be, thank you very much! Of course, such a mind-set does not preclude an afternoon lark to some distant monastery to see amusingly how some poor souls wish to spend their lives.

And you wonder why vocations to the monastery are slim?

Yet it is precisely the "artificial charade" that drives a few people to join monasteries and even more people to attach themselves in some way to a monastery. Only the "artificial charade" is not the monastery; it is the age, the culture, that is the artificial charade.

What attracts people to join or love the monastery? The monastery is real. It may be a difficult place to live one's life, but living one's life outside the monastery is difficult as well. The issue is not the degree of difficulty; the issue is the degree of reality in which the world indulges.

Many people are beginning to see the world becoming unreal. Of those people who are beginning to see the world in such a way, some—though not a lot—choose to live where they see reality: the monastery. More of the people who are beginning to see the world becoming unreal cannot—or will not—seek to live in a monastery, but they nevertheless want, perhaps even need, to be attached in some way to the monastery. Why? The monastery provides an island of reality in a world that is increasingly becoming unreal. Kardong ponders, "Monastic

---

[4] Bernhard A. Eckerstorfer, "The Challenge of Postmodernity to Monasticism," in *Church, Society and Monasticism: Acts of the International Symposium, Rome, May 31–June 3, 2006*, ed. Eduardo López-Tello García and Benedetta Selene Zorsi (Rome: Pontificio Ateneo S. Anselmo, 2009), 111 (Eckerstorfer's emphasis).

guesthouses are fuller than ever, but it is not always clear why people go there. Of course they are looking for quiet and order and peace . . . but there are all kinds of other retreats that offer those things, and they are not monastic."[5]

What makes the monastery real? The division of the day into liturgical prayer, *lectio*, and work within a community that fosters silence as well as fellowship. Ptacek notes that the monastery "brings order" to one's life.

I am not so naïve as to believe that monasteries are a paradise; however, what I am saying is that monasteries at least *strive* to be real as opposed to being artificial, a charade.

Which brings us back to Merton and his "danger of education." Merton rails against education being a "mass production," enabling graduates to participate in the artificial charade *without* really educating them to recognize and think critically. By *think critically* I mean the ability to take a set of variables and draw a logical conclusion. The ability to connect the dots.

For sure, educators love to talk about teaching their students to "think critically." But as any teacher knows, doing so is an uphill climb . . . in sand. Not because students are stupid, but because our age, our culture, does not really prize it. So why should they? What our age, our culture, prizes is mastery of facts. You want to think? Think on your own time. Meanwhile just give me the facts.

This is precisely the opposite of the monastery. In the monastery one can think, because space and time and silence are provided to do it. That's what makes it real. Benedict pleaded with his monks to listen. But you can't listen in a din, and if you can't listen you can't think.

An everyday example of what I'm talking about: One year a group of us teachers drove up from the north suburbs of

[5] Terrence Kardong, "Thoughts on the Future of Western Monasticism," in *A Monastic Vision for the 21st Century: Where Do We Go from Here?* ed. Patrick Hart, MW 8 (Kalamazoo, MI: Cistercian Publications, 2006), 62.

Chicago to Milwaukee in order to eat dinner at a restaurant called Mader's. We took two cars. I was driving one of the cars; two of my colleagues were with me. Soon after school was out for the day we drove to Milwaukeeland.

A few miles from the restaurant we encountered a detour due to road construction or a crash, I can't remember. We were still on the interstate, though. Anyway, the detour seemed to route us in the entirely wrong direction. The restaurant was one way, but the detour was taking us in the opposite direction. Furthermore, the phone we were using to help us arrive at our destination was telling us to take the detour. So I took the detour.

Wrong. The detour took us in completely the wrong direction. Somehow through sheer luck—not to mention through clenched teeth and muttered expletives—I managed to get us back onto the interstate near the point of the detour. But this time I didn't take the detour; I kept going in the direction I had plotted out using Mr. Rand McNally.

We arrived at Mader's ten minutes later.

There were three college-educated men in the car that day, and we listened to a phone.

My point: be careful who, or what, you listen to.

William of Saint-Thierry wrote in his *Golden Epistle*,

> It is for others to serve God, it is for you to cling to him; it is for others to believe in God, know him, love him, and revere him; it is for you to taste him, understand him, be acquainted with him, enjoy him.[6]

Notice the verbs: *cling, taste, understand, enjoy*. That is the key to the Christian life. William may have been setting up a dichotomy between monks and those who don't live in monasteries, but those verbs zero in on the heart of the matter.

---

[6] William of St. Thierry, *The Golden Epistle*, trans. Theodore Berkeley, CF 12 (Kalamazoo, MI: Cistercian Publications, 1971), 14.

Monks know this (presumably); those of us who don't live in monasteries suspect it. That's why those of us who don't live in monasteries want to go there. Who doesn't want to taste God? Michael Casey notes, "The key factor in the renewal of monastic life is its effectiveness in helping newcomers understand more fully the music in their souls."[7] Exactly. Monasticism isn't catechism but song. H. L. Mencken, no friend to Christianity, noted that decades ago when he wrote, "Religion is not a syllogism, but a poem."[8] The parish thunders "obey God!" The monastery says "experience God." Hence cling, taste, and enjoy.

WARNING: there can be no oblates or lay associates, however, without there being monks.

---

[7] Michael Casey, "Monasticism: Present and Future: Part II," *American Benedictine Review* 65, no. 3 (2014): 301.

[8] H. L. Mencken, *The Vintage Mencken* (New York: Vintage Books, 1955), 138.

Faith

Faith is not a feeling. Faith may very well produce intense feelings, but that is not faith. Faith is a gift from God in the form of consent to love, trust, and follow God. The object of faith is unseen (Heb 11:1) but anchored in reason and hope.

Faith is a journey, but a journey that is not linear. Faith is not geometry. The journey is not from point A to point B but an exploration of the depths of the human heart to discover the image and likeness of God, peel away the sin that has tarnished that image and likeness, rest there, and ultimately transcend the self. In this journey one can never dig too deep. Nor can one ever reach the bottom, for love—on which faith is based—is unfathomable.

The journey may seemingly veer off the path. This is an illusion. On the journey of faith, one can never veer off the path provided one remains on the journey. This is so because the path includes all those sins and moments of doubt we mistakenly believe push us off the path. The only way to be off the path is not to be on the journey in the first place. The end of the journey can never be foreseen. For it to be otherwise would be not faith but knowledge. God asks not for our knowledge but for our love, which is the root of faith. Time cannot confine faith. It is never too late to embrace faith—just consider the Good Thief (Luke 23:39-43).

Faith may wane, but probably it is fervor that wanes; the two are not the same. The zeal of freshly found faith is white hot, but when plunged into the waters of life—well, routine and familiarity quickly cool zeal. What remains is faith shorn of pretense, sentimentality, or dogma, and the soul stands naked before God, who asks, "What will it be?" And the universe hangs in the balance, for faith is about answering that question. Sirach puts it this way: *Before each person are life and death; whichever one chooses shall be given* (Sir 15:17).

On answering the question, the soul walks with God through a vast darkness, though this walk feels as though it is being made without God. Without the crutch of creed or code the soul gropes blindly for God, who has—paradoxically—been right there all along.

Faith cannot be generated, only accepted. Attempts to foster faith by pious thoughts, lengthy prayers, or increased church attendance are doomed to failure. One cannot impose oneself on God, nor can one purchase God's favor. Clamping down and vowing through clenched teeth, "I will have faith!" will not work. Faith is openness to God, not demands on him. William of Saint-Thierry wrote,

> They who possess the joy of the Lord may preach it and commend it to those who do not possess it. They may advise them how to seek it and tell them a way to recover it; and sometimes even, if grace is present, the will may be moved and desire excited. But this joy is tasted only by him into whom it pours itself. No one ascends this summit unless it bends down to him; no one feels this good unless it conforms him to itself; no one lives by this life unless it imparts itself to him.[1]

Faith is not intellectual assent to creeds or dogmas. Rather, creed and dogma flow from faith. Abraham followed God, not the Torah. As Scripture notes, *Abram put his faith in the Lord, who credited it to him as an act of righteousness* (Gen 15:6). Peter walked across the water not to embrace creed but to embrace Christ (Matt 14:28-29). In other words, faith is fixed on God.

---

[1] William of St. Thierry, *Exposition on the Song of Songs* 7.202, trans. Columba Hart, CF 6 (Kalamazoo, MI: Cistercian Publications, 1970), 162.

Faith precedes creed. Creed and dogma are certainly important, for they point the way to Christ, but creed and dogma
are not the Way. Only Jesus is the Way. William makes the
difference clear:

> Know yourself, then, to be my image; thus you can know
> me, whose image you are, and you will find me within you.
> If you are with me in your soul, there I will repose with you;
> and then I will feed you. . . .
>
> Be wholly present to yourself, therefore, and employ your-
> self wholly in knowing yourself and knowing whose image
> you are, and likewise in discerning and understanding what
> you are and what you can do in him whose image you are.[2]

The image is found with the individual (Gen 1:27; 2:7; Luke
17:21). The task of the Christian is to discover, encounter,
and love the image who resides within himself or herself.
Doing so, the Christian transcends the self, so becoming able
to fulfill the law of God: love God and neighbor as Christ
loves—unconditionally.

To recapture the image of God is to be made holy by God.
Thus we strive not to be good but to be holy (Lev 19:2; 1 Pet
1:16). A pagan can be good. The atheist can be a good upstand-
ing member of the community. But the Christian aspires to be
holy. Saint Gregory of Nyssa wrote,

> Blessedness does not lie in knowing something about God,
> but rather in possessing God within oneself. . . . Those who
> look at the sun in a mirror, even if they do not look directly
> at the sky, see its radiance in the reflection just as truly as do
> those who look directly at the sun's orb. It is the same, says
> the Lord, with you. Even though you are unable to contem-
> plate and see the inaccessible light, you will find what you

---

[2] William, *Exposition* 5.63, 66; CF 6:51, 53.

seek within yourself, provided you return to the beauty and grace of that image which was originally placed in you.[3]

Some Christians are wary of the idea of finding God within the self, believing that to do so smacks of New Age thought. The Christian, however, does not worship the self. The self is renewed through Christ. Merton put it this way:

> To know ourselves is the basis of all our meditation and our prayer, not in the sense that we are the ultimate end of all our investigations (God preserve us from such a doom), but we come to know God through knowing his image which is planted in the depth and center and in the very substance of our souls.[4]

By loving God, by being totally consumed by God, the self disappears into union with God. Not that the self becomes God, but that the self can no longer be known apart from God, cannot even be seen apart from God. Those who accomplish this we call saints.

Love is the response to the encounter with the image. What bridegroom does not feel a pang of love on seeing his bride? What bride on seeing her bridegroom does not have longing for him? The encounter between God and his image is the same. We cannot see God face to face (this side of existence, anyway), nor can our finite minds contain the infinite God. We can, however, know God by loving God. Again, William of Saint-Thierry writes, "For love of God is itself knowledge of him; unless he is loved, he is not known, and unless he is known, he is not loved. He is known only insofar as he is loved, and he is loved only insofar as he is known."[5]

---

[3] Gregory of Nyssa, Oratio 6, *De beatitudinibus*, PG 44:1270–71, in *The Liturgy of the Hours* (New York: Catholic Book Publishing Co., 1976), 3:413–14.

[4] Thomas Merton, "Blessed William of Saint-Thierry: Monk of Signy," *Cistercian Studies Quarterly* 35, no. 1 (2000): 8.

[5] William of St. Thierry, *Exposition* 7.76; CF 6:64.

Faith, then, is love of God. Faith is not love of rules about God. It is not mere happenstance that love is the denominator. Jesus said that to inherit everlasting life one must love—love God and neighbor (Luke 10:25-28), and love others as he loves us (John 15:12). That's it. John whittled all theology down to a simple equation: God is love (1 John 4:8, 16). If love is the very definition of God, then love trumps everything, for God trumps everything. Saint Paul flat out champions the primacy of love: *So faith, hope, and love remain, these three; but the greatest of these is love* (1 Cor 13:13).

The union of one to God can never be exhausted. Love for God, unity with God, can always grow stronger, run deeper, burn brighter. William of Saint-Thierry writes, "No longer does it [the heart] merely desire what God desires, not only does it love him, but it is perfect in its love, so that it can will only what God wills."[6]

Humanity cannot be what it was created to be without loving God. Abraham Joshua Heschel wrote,

> Man treats himself as if he were created in the likeness of a machine rather than in the likeness of God. The body is his god, and its needs are his prophets. Having lost his awareness of his sacred image, he became deaf to the meaning: to live in a way which is compatible with his image.[7]

It is sometimes said of a film that "it was so bad it was good." Faith is the same way: it is so simple that it is difficult. All one needs to do is accept it. Yet we continually categorize it, codify it. We do so because we believe that something so wonderful and grand can only come in a package of gold and silk, can only be approached through arcane systems of

[6] William of St. Thierry, *The Golden Epistle* 15.257, trans. Theodore Berkeley, CF 12 (Kalamazoo, MI: Cistercian Publications, 1980), 94.

[7] Abraham Joshua Heschel, *The Insecurity of Freedom* (Philadelphia: Jewish Publication Society of America, 1966), 12.

thought. We complicate that which is simple. The Magi before the infant Jesus is a good example. The Magi bring gifts fit for a king, yet the King presents himself as a helpless infant. The gifts of the Magi are rare and expensive items, but the Lord asks only to be loved.

The journey of faith requires a lifetime. No matter if one lives one hundred years or half that or even half that: one is always *becoming* in the faith. No one ever arrives, because the depths of God can never be reached. Therefore, faith can never be complete or have an end. Faith is a mysterious and some-times frustrating journey, but all that is ever asked of us is *if today you hear God's voice, harden not your hearts* (Heb 3:15).

The monk attempts, every day, to hear God's voice.

Prayer

Prayer is the language of faith. Faith is the love we have for God, and prayer is the expression of that love. As with any language, the language of prayer must be learned. One might protest by saying that true prayer "comes from the heart" and should be "spontaneous." Prayer can certainly well up spontaneously, and that is truly good. However, to consign prayer only to the level of spontaneity is like saying a two-year-old can speak fluently.

Monks know this. The daily cycle of offices ensures it.

In order to learn to pray one must practice (see above sentence). One does not learn to play the piano by listening to piano music. In order to learn to pray, one must pray. That may seem self-evident. But wait until the time comes when you do not feel like praying. Like the student learning to play the piano, you must practice prayer even when the mood to do so is not there.

You who are married know this. You sometimes do things you don't want to do for the sake of a strong marriage. Your spouse does the same for you. Prayer is no different.

For, like faith, prayer is not a matter of feeling or mood. Prayer may evoke strong emotions, but that is not prayer. Anyone who has practiced prayer for the least amount of time knows that the very desire for prayer is a gift from God. It is not something we conjure up ourselves. Not that prayer is or should be drudgery, but the time will arise when one does not feel like praying. That time, however, is not an excuse to refrain from prayer.

Prayer is not so much a decision to pray as it is a surrender to God. It is an emptying of the self. Prayer is letting go, the realization that we are not in control, but that God is. As Michael Casey notes, we don't even produce prayer; God does.[1] We merely allow it to wash over us. In prayer the ego dies and the true self cleaves to God. Because prayer is about surrender, because prayer is about denying the self, prayer is the antithesis of rugged individualism. Prayer is the opposite of being in control.

Prayer deepens in proportion to the degree to which we die to self and cleave to God. In prayer we stand naked before God; we are exposed. Thus we come to understand that we are totally dependent on God. Jesus' crucifixion is the example of perfect prayer. *My God, my God, why have you forsaken me?* Jesus cries (Mark 15:34). No answer comes forth. Through all that, though, Jesus trusts in his Father; he still clings to God in his darkest hour.

Such is the level of prayer for which we strive: that we may cling to God in the face of silence and darkness. To cling to the belief that God is Emmanuel—God with us—even in times of such darkness takes, well, faith. Just ask Saint Mother Teresa.

Silence is the sound of prayer, which is why, I think, monks are keen on silence. Silence is at the same time both the milieu of prayer and the mode of prayer. Silence calms our souls and quiets our thoughts. Not that we try to suppress our thoughts during prayer. Can't be done. Rather, while in prayer we simply want to avoid distractions.

Prayer is like sitting on a riverbank. We come to the riverbank to watch the river—the water—drift by. We allow the lazy current of the river to lull us. Now and then a piece of driftwood slips by. Maybe a barge lumbers along. We notice it, but we don't dwell on it. Anyhow, those things soon disappear into the distance. But the river is still there. What's important is the river, not the driftwood, not the barge.

[1] Michael Casey, *Toward God: The Ancient Wisdom of Western Prayer* (Liguori, MO: Liguori/Triumph, 1996), 33.

Now while you're sitting on that riverbank, even if you are with someone, you notice that words are superfluous. What you want to concentrate on is the river. Well, prayer is no different. The deeper you descend into the silence of prayer and the longer you rest in God, the more you realize that words are a waste. Prayer is not about words; it's about listening. "But Jesus taught us to pray the words of the Our Father," you might say. Have you ever noticed how short that prayer is? It's short and to the point. Not verbose in the least. We are to pray the words and then *listen*.

Silence, all people, in the presence of the Lord (Zech 2:17); *but the Lord is in his holy temple; silence before him, all the earth* (Hab 2:20); *be still and know that I am God* (Ps 46:11); *be still before the Lord; wait for God* (Ps 37:7).

Thus prayer can be summed up as follows: get in, get out, shut up, sit down (actually that's my prime directive in regard to homilies, but it works here, too).

Prayer is not about concepts. It is about entering the mystery of God, who is beyond all concepts. The anonymous fourteenth-century author of *The Cloud of Unknowing* wrote,

> It is equally useless to think you can nourish your contemplative work by considering God's attributes, his kindness or his dignity; or by thinking about Our Lady, the angels, or the saints; or about heaven, wonderful as these will be. It is far better to let your mind rest in awareness of him in his naked existence and to love and praise him for what he is in himself.[2]

Consider two people making love—do they think about all the ways they love their spouse? Do they consult a manual? Of course not. They are lost in the moment of making love. Prayer is the same. It's not in the concepts; it's resting in the doing.

---

[2] *The Cloud of Unknowing*, trans. William Johnston (New York: Doubleday, 1973), 54.

This resting silently and wordlessly in the presence of God has a name: contemplation. Contemplation as described here—silently and wordlessly resting in God free of concepts—is an ancient form of Christian prayer. It rests steadfastly in the Christian tradition. This tradition stretches back beyond the fourteenth century of *The Cloud of Unknowing* to the Desert Fathers and Mothers of Egypt and Syria in the fourth century. Evagrius, Cassian, Antony all practiced contemplation.

In *The Chapters on Prayer* Evagrius, born in AD 345 in what is now Turkey, wrote "Stand guard over your spirit, keep it free of concepts at the time of prayer so that it may remain in its own calm"; "Do not by any means strive to fashion some image or visualize some form at the time of prayer"; "Happy is the spirit that attains to perfect formlessness at the time of prayer"; and "Happy is the spirit that attains to complete unconsciousness of all sensible experience at the time of prayer."[3]

These aphorisms, composed sometime between 390 and 395, are the heart of monastic prayer. Such prayer helps us to probe the depths of our center in order to discover and rest in God. Once at this center, the Christian is liberated from the self so that what remains is God. *Not* that we become God, but that God consumes our being. All this is done in an atmosphere of silence and calm. Cassian put it this way:

> This prayer centers on no contemplation of some image or other. It is masked by no attendant sounds or words. It is a fiery outbreak, an indescribable exaltation, an insatiable thrust of the soul. Free of what is sensed and seen, ineffable in its groans and sighs, the soul pours itself out to God.[4]

Such forms of prayer sound odd or exotic to some modern Christians who prefer vocal or mental prayer. It is not that

[3] Evagrius Ponticus, *The Praktikos[;] Chapters on Prayer*, trans. John Eudes Bamberger, CS 4 (Kalamazoo, MI: Cistercian Publications, 1972), 66–75.

[4] John Cassian, *Conferences*, trans. Colm Luibheid, Classics of Western Spirituality (Mahwah, NJ: Paulist Press, 1985), 138.

contemplation is better than other forms of prayer. It is to say, however, that contemplation is a traditional form of Christian prayer.

Basil Pennington noted that monasteries should be "places where persons can go to learn contemplative meditation just as the Buddhist monasteries and centers are."[5] How sad that children educated in any Christian school would believe that only Buddhists practice contemplation. If the exotic is what you seek, you can't go wrong exploring ancient Christian wisdom from guys named John the Dwarf, Isaac of the Cells, Poemen the Shepherd, or Paul the Simple.

Prayer is not about technique, however. Contemplation is not some mathematical equation through which, once it is solved, you automatically find God. Contemplation is not a riddle to ponder and, having put all the pieces together, presto! You see God. Contemplation is not a method, but an attitude; not a gadget, but a way of life.

This way of life is lived in humility. Humility is the knowledge that you have been created in God's image and that your life is not your own (1 Cor 6:19). Pride seeks to make God appear after having pushed all the right buttons, after calculating the proper formulas, after saying the prescribed prayers over a predetermined span of time. Pride wants God to conform to you. Humility is surrender to God. Humility understands that one's virtue springs not from self but from God. Humility seeks union with God in a life lived in tranquility and love, in a life that transcends the self. The proud demand God's appearance; the humble cry for God's embrace.

In the end, then, prayer is not something you do; nor is contemplation something distinct from prayer. Prayer becomes the way you live your life. Prayer and your life become one and the same. Contemplation and life meld into the arms of God, and the self disappears. All that remains is God.

---

[5] M. Basil Pennington, "The Benedictine Contribution to Evangelization," *American Benedictine Review* 49, no. 2 (1998): 228.

Scripture

Here is the way I learned the Bible growing up in the Baptist Church: The Sunday School teacher gave us a list of verses to memorize, usually in sets of ten. If you memorized all ten verses, you received a treat of some sort (candy bar, baseball cards). Once you had successfully memorized those ten, another set of ten was given. This is how you were tested to see if you had the verses memorized: the Sunday School teacher would say, "Mark, recite for me John 3:16." And I would have to recite it. Or she (the Sunday School teacher was always a woman) might recite John 3:16 herself and then ask me to provide the book, chapter, and verse of the passage she had just recited to me. The most I ever memorized was six. Girls always memorized the most. (The champion in the last Sunday School class I attended at First Baptist Church was a girl who memorized fifty verses. I don't know what treat she received.)

Scripture is the passage to prayer. In the days before the printing press, when the Bible had to be copied by hand, copies were few. Most folks did not have easy access to the Bible either to read or to consult. Furthermore, many people in the time before the printing press were unable to read. So even if one had access to a copy of the Bible, such access did not guarantee that one could read it. Consequently, some people of this time tended to memorize large chunks of the Bible. Either through reading passages themselves, or having passages from the Bible read to them, people mulled over passages of Scripture until they learned them by heart.

Memorization and knowing by heart are not synonymous. I have memorized telephone numbers, my Social Security number, and e-mail addresses. I use those numbers every day, and I do not have to make an effort to bring them to mind. The numbers or the addresses are purely functional; I punch in the telephone number and, seconds later, I'm talking to someone. The number I used to access the person is meaningless as soon as the person with whom I wish to speak comes on the line.

When I was a child my dad read me Longfellow's "The Wreck of the Hesperus." He read me other Longfellow poems, but that is the one I remember. I can still recite a chunk of it (from the beginning through the line, "And a scornful laugh laughed he").

In elementary school we had to memorize Lincoln's Gettysburg Address. I got about halfway through.

I'm a big James Joyce fan. At one time I had the whole last section of his short story "The Dead" memorized, from the line "She was fast asleep" to the conclusion of the story, a little over seven hundred words. Great stuff.

But all that was memorized: mere words.

On the other hand, some of the psalms I know by heart. These words are not just stored in my head; they live in my heart. When I bring them to mind, the words are not merely recited as if they were Longfellow's poem. No, the psalms I know by heart are chewed and gnawed upon so that I can digest them. They are internalized and mulled over. The words of the psalms become part of my being. They create a passage, allowing me access to God. The words are prayer. I don't need a book; it's in my heart.

Monasticism has a special tradition with Scripture, with reading. Michael Casey writes that the "Benedictine tradition is a literary tradition."[1] That tradition is based primarily on *lectio divina*. First and foremost, *lectio* is prayer. In *lectio* you do not so much read Scripture as listen to it. Who are you listening to? God. *Lectio* is not an academic exercise. In *lectio* you do not

---

[1] Michael Casey, *The Art of Winning Souls: Pastoral Care of Novices*, MW 35 (Collegeville, MN: Cistercian Publications, 2012), 158.

read Scripture to argue theology or prove a point. *Lectio* is not about knowing God; it is about experiencing God.

Lectio is not a devotional. In a devotional, the person is active, petitioning or beseeching God. The line of action goes from person to God. *Lectio* is just the opposite: God comes to the person and the person listens.

Lectio begins with reverence for the Word. You have to come to the prayer of *lectio* with the belief that Scripture is the word of God, that God not only *is* speaking to you through Scripture but *wants* to speak to you in Scripture. *Lectio* is not the academic study of the Bible or a Bible study. In *lectio* you are trying to *listen* to God, not explain the text.

To do this, you do not simply grab a copy of the Bible, flop down in a chair, open the book, and immediately begin to plow through Paul. Before entering into *lectio*, you cut yourself off from where you have just been by going to another room, or leaving the house entirely, or stepping out into the quiet of the yard or a park. Before reading take some deep breaths. Pray for God's presence with, perhaps, the prayer, "Come, Holy Spirit, fill the hearts of your faithful, and enkindle in them the fire of your love." Light candles. The idea is that you pray *lectio* in some sort of space that is separate.

Well beforehand, know what passage you are going to pray. Once you begin, read slowly, preferably aloud. Reading aloud cuts down on distractions and helps internalize the words being read. There is something about words rolling off the tongue that gives them more impact than when you read those same words silently. Read until a word or phrase strikes you and then stop. Mull over the word or phrase. Allow it to seep into you. This rumination is prayer. This is the essence of *lectio*. Charles Cummings explains it this way:

> Sacred reading is a process of assimilating the word of God and letting its meaning spread through our blood into every part of our being, a process of impregnation, interiorization, personalization of the word of God. Yet the process is a

gentle one. . . . The encounter takes place without drama as we quietly savor and relish the mystery of God's caring presence. The encounter is real without being extraordinary or spectacular. . . .

The effects of sacred reading should become evident over a long period of time in a person's life. Repeated encounters with the word of God will bring about a gradual transformation as our thinking and willing become progressively harmonized with God's will. Slowly we grow in interior freedom and lose our innate orientation toward comfort and security.[2]

How much text is to be covered in one sitting? That is the beauty of *lectio*: there are no rules. Read as long and as far as the Spirit moves you to read. One time you may cover only a single verse. At another time maybe only half a verse. Still other times several verses. Several months may be required to read an entire book of the Bible. No Bible Police will bust down your door and throttle you for reading too few verses.

What is vital to *lectio* is persistence. You must pray this prayer routinely over a long period of time in order for it to have an effect. It must become a habit. Otherwise, the prayer is futile.

We bring no preconceived notions or agendas to this form of prayer. In *lectio* we welcome God into our hearts. The idea is to allow God to act on us by listening to God, as opposed to trying—vainly—to act on God. In praying the Scriptures we emulate Christ, who prayed the Scriptures, prayed them even when he was dying on the cross.

But *lectio* is contingent on something: faith in, and love for, the Bible. Such faith in and love for the Bible requires some sort of acquaintance with it. I know that sounds self-evident, but hear me out on this. Where does faith and love for the Bible come from? I have students who tell me the only copy of the

---

[2] Charles Cummings, *Monastic Practices*, rev. ed., MW 75 (Collegeville, MN: Cistercian Publications, 2015), 4.

Bible in their homes is a huge tome that sits on a bookcase. Well, that's a start.

Here's my context of Bible.

Back in the early 1980s, my mom, dad, and brother, his fiancée, my younger brother, Sara, and I are all at my parents' house. We are talking about my brother's approaching wedding. Specifically, my future sister-in-law is trying to persuade her future husband (my brother) that a certain passage from the Bible should be read at their upcoming wedding (Protestant). Unable actually to recall the Scripture passage she wants read, she asks my brother to bring her a Bible.

Dad guffaws, and all discourse grinds to a halt. Why? Because everyone in that house knows that finding a Bible there is analogous to finding kryptonite in the house. Everyone, that is, except the future bride.

Mom, in a desperate ploy to save face, assures us all that a copy of the Good Book can certainly be had, and she instructs my brother to hunt for it.

Minutes pass. My brother calls from down in the basement with a question. Dad hollers, "Try behind the bar!" Mom shoots daggers at Dad, who just shrugs. However, Dad knows exactly what he's doing. He knows that my brother's fiancée's family are teetotalers. He just did that to get in a dig.

More minutes pass. Finally, my brother appears back upstairs sans Bible. With her ever-present cigarette in hand and waving her arms in exasperation, my mother cries, "Oh, there's a Bible here someplace!"

My brother makes one last stab at it, but comes up short. Mom is clearly upset. Then my wife, Sara, chimes in, "Why don't we ask Ma?" Ma was what we called my grandmother, my mother's mother.

This is a real coup. All present know that Ma, a by-God Baptist, owns several copies of Holy Writ. Furthermore, she lives just down the street, and she can be at the house in no time. Finally, and more important, Ma is family. Hence, though a Bible might not be on the actual premises, a copy of the Bible is in the clutches of a dear family member, thus making Mom's claim to possessing a Bible one step closer to reality.

The call is made. Ma appears in a flash. Clutching the Bible. Upon Ma's arrival Mom stands, walks to her mother, takes the Bible from her, holds it aloft, and says oh so seriously—I kid you not—"See, here it is."

Is that a forehead slapper or what?

The key to that story is Mom's embarrassment that a Bible could not be found in the house. Why the embarrassment? I have only a hunch.

Though Mom rarely darkened the door of any church, she nevertheless understood propriety. She had listened to my brother describe, in glowing terms no less, the social status of his future bride. The status was not one of wealth or class. My brother's fiancée's family was no better off financially than my parents. Nor did she hail from a family with a prominent pedigree.

Rather, the status my mom zeroed in on was that the family her son was marrying into was well known and highly regarded in the Methodist Church. This rattled Mom, because our family never went to church. Her own mother, however, was very active in the First Baptist Church. Ma attended church every Sunday. She had once taught Sunday School. She attended Wednesday-night prayer meeting. Thus, when the issue of getting hold of a Bible sprang up, Mom wanted to save face in front of her future daughter-in-law. No, they never went to church, but they weren't so far gone as not even to have a Bible in the house.

My point is this: that embarrassment my mom experienced? I don't believe she would be embarrassed were that to happen today. How, then, is Bible supposed to be prayed if people don't even have a Bible?

I think this is where the monastery comes in. *Lectio* is the ideal prayer for people who are wary of, confused by, or afraid of the Bible. Ask students what races through their heads when they hear that they are going to read Bible in class: they can't pronounce those crazy names, they haven't a clue where all those towns are or how to say them, the language is strange and off-putting, they don't know what any of that stuff means.

But what if there were a method of reading Bible in which you could stay clear of the odd names and towns, where you didn't have to try to figure out what it meant? What if you didn't have to cover a certain block of text? What if there was no pressure to read a certain book of the Bible, starting at its beginning and reading to its end? And what if students were instructed *not* to read rapidly, but to read *slowly*?

That would be totally counterintuitive to high school students. All their academic life they have been trained to read a text for information, for facts. Scanning a text for relevant information has been the goal. Speed reading is a prized skill.

That is why students have such problems with *lectio* when they first begin this method. In *lectio* they are told not to scan, not to read quickly, not to search out facts and information. They are told to slow down. To slow down! They are told that they are not in ultimate control of their reading; they are told God is in control. You see a lot of bewildered faces when you introduce this method. Not until the semester is coming to a close does the method begin to resonate with the students.

So how does *lectio* play out in the classroom?

In my Catholic spirituality class (seniors only), each class begins with either Morning Prayer or Evening Prayer from the Liturgy of the Hours (the slim volume titled *Shorter Christian Prayer*). If the class meets before lunch, we pray Morning Prayer. If the class meets after lunch, we pray Evening Prayer. Before commencing either prayer, I instruct the students to open their Bibles to the point where they left off in their *lectio* during the previous class. I also instruct the students to get out their *lectio* notebook and pens. I require each student to keep such a notebook in which to write down the word or phrase that struck them during *lectio*. I check these notebooks weekly. Frankly, this is a means for me to ensure the students are complying with my instructions. However, as I explain to the students, at the end of the semester they will have compiled their very own prayer book, which they can consult at any time.

The Liturgy of the Hours usually lasts ten minutes. I then allow another ten minutes for *lectio.* Thus, in a seventy-minute class, the first twenty minutes or so are totally devoted to prayer, leaving approximately fifty minutes for remaining classroom work.

Ten minutes may sound skimpy. However, when the students first begin praying *lectio*, that ten minutes seems very long to them. As the semester progresses, though, those ten minutes seem to grow shorter, at least for most students. Remember what is trying to be accomplished here and the audience. The goal is to introduce eighteen-year-olds to a habit of listening to God the Father through his Christ the Word.

Reading the biblical text, not reading *about* the biblical text, is crucial. Students cannot become lovers of the text unless they actually read the text. A lover wants to savor the experience of his or her beloved. The same goes for the Bible.

Raymond Studzinski, a Benedictine monk at Saint Meinrad Archabbey, writes, "The Scriptures provided the monastic reader not with logical arguments . . . but with a sacred narrative that would lead the reader to wisdom."[3] Don't we all want wise students?

So I looked to Jean Leclercq for this idea. He writes about the Scriptures:

> The basic method [of reading Scripture] is different from that of non-monastic circles where Scripture is read, namely the schools. Originally, *lectio divina* and *sacra pagina* are equivalent expressions. For St. Jerome as for St. Benedict, the *lectio divina* is the text itself. . . . During the Middle Ages, this expression was to be reserved more and more for

[3] Raymond Studzinski, *Reading to Live: The Evolving Practice of* Lectio Divina, CS 231 (Collegeville, MN: Cistercian Publications, 2009), 15.

the act of reading, "the reading of Holy Scripture." In the School it refers most often to the page itself, the text which is under study, taken objectively. Scripture is studied for its own sake. In the cloister, however, it is rather the reader and the benefit that he derives from Holy Scripture which are given consideration. In both instances an activity is meant which is "holy," *sacra, divina*; but in the two milieus, the accent is put on two different aspects of the same activity. The orientation differs, and, consequently, so does the procedure. The scholastic *lectio* takes the direction of the *quaestio* and the *disputatio*. The reader puts questions to the text and then questions himself on the subject matter: *quaeri solet*. The monastic *lectio* is oriented toward the *meditatio* and the *oratio*. The objective of the first is science and knowledge; of the second, wisdom and appreciation. In the monastery, the *lectio divina*, this activity which begins with grammar, terminates in compunction, in desire for heaven.[4]

So I thought, why not apply that line of thinking to my classroom? Why not bring a component of the cloister to the classroom? In my freshman Old and New Testament classes, the goal is to pass on the story and to cultivate a Christian vocabulary. With the seniors the goal is to help them learn to listen to God and to instill in them the desire for God.

Imitate the monks, people. They've been around a long time. I think they know what they're doing.

---

[4] Jean Leclercq, *The Love of Learning and the Desire for God: A Study of Monastic Culture*, trans. Catherine Misrahi, 2nd ed. (New York: Fordham University Press, 2007), 72.

Oak Barrels

Bourbon is an acquired taste.

Forty years ago, when I was first married, I received a bottle of Maker's Mark as a gift. I recall pouring a shot glass to nearly the brim and knocking it back. Burn! It took me, literally, ten years to empty that bottle.

Today? Not nearly so long to empty a bottle.

Whether or not that is a good thing is debatable. What is not debatable, I think, is that you should work yourself up to enjoying bourbon.

Thus I believe it best to introduce your taste buds with a spirit of low proof, say Basil Hayden (distilled by Beam in Clermont, Kentucky). It is bottled at eighty-proof (meaning that the alcohol content is 40 percent), and the spirit is light, almost gentle. The burn factor is minimal. As your taste for the spirit evolves, other brands of higher proof can be more easily imbibed. This is not to say that lower-proof bourbons such as Basil Hayden are of inferior quality. They are not. But a bourbon novice belting back a higher-proof spirit from the get-go is risking being turned off to the spirit way too soon.

Not long ago my brother Mike slipped me a bottle of George T. Stagg, Antique Collection (distilled by Buffalo Trace, just outside of Frankfort, Kentucky). Aged fifteen years. 138.2 proof (69 percent alcohol). Purchase price in the three figures. Poured me two fingers (neat) and sniffed it. Good aroma. Sipped it. Oh, man! Nectar of the gods! I nursed that bottle for as long as I could. Imbibed only on special occasions (Christmas, Easter, July 4).

When I finally finished the bottle I drove to Binny's and bought a popular brand of bourbon priced around twenty dollars, give or take (Stagg is out of my price range). Took it home, poured myself a couple of fingers, and retreated to the patio to watch the sun go down. Wretched. Could hardly get it down. The only reason I didn't toss it was that I would have felt guilty pouring it on the freshly mowed grass.

Moral of the story: once you develop a taste for the really good stuff, going back to the more pedestrian stuff can be a real trial.

What has this got to do with anything? Well, this—monasticism is like a good bourbon: once you have imbibed the monastery, going back to the run-of-the-mill parish stuff is ho-hum.

The monastery has the good stuff: liturgy, *lectio*, silence, and community. The pace is slower. In fact, time is a factor at the monastery. One does not become a full-fledged monk as soon as one passes into the cloister. Five or six years pass before being fully admitted into the house. In other words, the person must age, mature in the life, before being fully admitted. Bourbon ages in oak barrels; monks age in the cell. Those oak barrels are charred by fire before the newly distilled bourbon is poured into them. The succeeding seasons of heat and cold draw and expel the bourbon into and out of the wood. That cycle gives the bourbon its flavor and color. The longer the bourbon is aged, the better it will taste, the deeper the color. The monk ages in the fires of obedience and stability, but most of all in the battle against the self. The greatest fire is learning to be configured to Christ, not to oneself. The longer one remains in the monastery, the greater the odds of transcending the self and configuring the self to Christ. Time is the monk's best friend.

When a bourbon has been aged a long time, say fifteen to eighteen years or more, when that barrel is finally opened, it is highly possible that only two or three gallons of bourbon remain. Now you know why good hooch costs an arm and a leg.

The monastery is no different. Time takes a toll on the women and men who inhabit the monastery, and many leave. Those who remain are few.

God, bourbon, and psalms on a steamy hot evening along the Indiana side of the Ohio River fifteen miles downstream from Louisville, Kentucky. Humidity so high you need gills to breathe. Sweat oozing from every pore. That angry ol' sun has finally dipped behind the hills, and now the haze is beginning to fall all fat and sassy on the mighty, muddy water.

The Ohio River! That powerful muscle of water that slices Indiana and Kentucky in two, brown gurgling water nearly a mile wide where I'm standing. A mother to barges and mystery and dreams. *Let the rivers clap their hands!* says Psalm 98:8. This river complies with the Lord!

And desolate. You want desolation? Drive where I am standing right now: Indiana Highway 111 south. South of the Highway 211 cutoff is isolation. Hardly a house for miles and miles. The river will be on your left as you drive south. Curtains of trees obscure the view of the water, but then wham! A clearing in the trees! The river flashes into view, and the sight is at once mysterious and powerful.

Don't you see? That's God speaking! Where no one is, where no one wants to be, where this wonderful water rolls by unobserved. There God dwells. I, along the riverbank, and that eagle that glides high above the river are the only ones to see it. So be it.

O Lord, how short is the length of my days. Now I know how fleeting is my life (Ps 39:5). God in his mercy, however, has blessed me. How blessed I am to see what I see! How blessed I am to be so deep in a land that I am hidden from view, save God's. It is as if God has enveloped me in his arms and is holding me close to his bosom. A land no one wants. A land teeming with angels and the footprint of God. A land city folk mock and ignore. Good! More opportunity for me to experience this blessing.

Inhale deeply. My lungs fill with the odor of water and mud and sweat and dew. I sit down in it, because I must feel it. And all the while the water rolls by. I watch it. Listen to it. It has a language, you know. Then, a screech of that eagle sailing above.

This river doesn't boast. It doesn't need to. This river is confident, because this river is doing the will of God. All I can do is accept what I see, hear, and smell, and be thankful to God who gave me the opportunity to experience it, revel in it. What does the prophet Daniel say? *Deliver us by your wonders, and bring glory to your name, O Lord* (Dan 3:43). If this river isn't wondrous, my name is Burl Grundy. If I'm not being delivered by experiencing this wonder, then damned I am.

The glory is in the simplicity: a river, an eagle, and silence. That's it. Bernard got it right back in the twelfth century when he wrote,

> Be simple with your Lord . . ., putting away not only all guile and simulation, but equally all multiplicity of occupation, so that you may converse freely with him whose voice is so sweet and face so comely.[1]

This river harbors no guile.

Real presence? You want to talk real presence? I defy anyone to say God is not walking here. *The waters saw you, O God, the waters saw you and trembled* (Ps 77:17), and *It stretched out its branches to the sea, to the Great River it stretched out its shoots* (Ps 80:12).

Here I taste God as assuredly as I taste Eucharist. I may not be in church, but I am with God here on this water. I shout

---

[1] Bernard, S 43.7; *Sancti Bernardi Opera*, ed. Jean Leclercq, et al. (Rome: Editiones Cistercienses, 1968), 5.243; "Sermon on the Solemnity of the Assumption 3.7," trans. Irene Edmonds, CF 54 (Collegeville, MN: Cistercian Publications, 2016), 31–32; translation here from John R. Sommerfeldt, *Bernard of Clairvaux: On the Spirituality of Relationship* (New York: Newman Press, 2004), 18.

with joy and praise that God has touched me, that God has allowed me to savor his sweetness. *Taste and see that the Lord is good* (Ps 34:9).

Downstream I see it: a barge, three wide. At first it's only a speck on the water. Slowly, it lumbers forth, silent and stealthy. The barge is hugging the Indiana side of the river, already anticipating the approach to the locks on the Kentucky side upriver in Louisville. Finally, the barge is opposite me. I wave and let out a yell. The barge blasts its horn in reply. For several minutes I watch it chug its way upstream, wondering what its destination is.

My destination is God's face. But as that barge drifts out of sight into the haze of a hot, humid evening, I ask myself, will I see God's face? Or will I obscure God's face with the haze of sin?

I was born on the banks of this river six decades ago. In my time I have been blessed to dive into the depths of the Almighty, and in my sinfulness God has cleansed me in the waters of baptism, which, to me, is this river of God.

Don't monks experience the same thing in the cloister? Am I not imitating them? Tell me I'm wrong.

Twelve-year-old bourbon tastes mighty good on nights like this.

PART THREE

Telos

Forest, Indiana

Pull out Mr. Rand McNally's Road Atlas and turn to the state of Indiana. Find Indianapolis (hint: middle of the state). Now slide your finger straight up, following US Highway 31. When your finger reaches State Highway 26 (if you reach Kokomo you've gone too far), drag your finger to the left, oh, say nine miles, until you see the town of Middlefork. There, right underneath Middlefork, you will see a little speck of a town: Forest, Indiana.

That's what I want to talk about.

At the southeastern corner of the intersection of County Road 600N and County Road 880E sits a ranch house made of stone. The front of the house faces west, and a covered porch is between the attached garage to the north of the porch and the remaining length of the house to the south. The driveway, once blacktop, is now pulverized pebbles.

The house has three bedrooms and one full bath. A toilet, sink, and small shower are off the master bedroom. The family room juts off the north end of the kitchen. Sliding doors, facing east, are in the eat-in kitchen.

To the south of the house is a pole barn, complete with an office on the east end.

The house, built around 1960, sits on two acres and a crawl space. Septic and well; totally electric. No gas line to the house. One early spring an ice storm brought down power lines. Laird and Sue Jacoby, my in-laws who lived in the house, didn't have power or heat or a cooking mechanism for over a week.

They lived in this house from the late 1980s to 2012.

On the east and south the house is surrounded by farm fields. County Road 800E runs in front of the house, and on the other side of that county road, more farm fields stretch west. The surrounding farm fields rotate crops. One year corn, the next year beans. Bordering the north end of the property is a large lawn of the neighboring house to the northeast.

Mature white pines hug the northern exposure of the house. Yellow pine needles litter the roof of the house in fall. Yes, the gutters get clogged. Another row of mature pine trees stretches along the east side of the house, oh, about twenty-five yards from the back door. From that point, the remaining property rolls east about a hundred yards until abutting the neighbor's field of corn or beans.

The house is about a quarter of a mile from the edge of Forest, population 839 in 2000. The town's main drag runs east–west. There is a post office. There is a garage that specializes in servicing small farm equipment. A rusty old railroad track, defunct and with weeds towering through the rotted ties, divides Forest nearly evenly east–west. There is an abandoned grain elevator. You need to go either to nearby Michigantown or Russiaville or Frankfort (where there is a Walmart) to buy food.

The air in Forest smells of earth, dung, and fertilizer.

Forest sits in the northeast corner of Clinton County. Frankfort is the seat of the county. The nickname of Frankfort High School? The Hotdogs. The county is smack-dab in farm country. Unlike southern Indiana, the earth in Clinton County is black.

At night, if the sky is clear, the stars . . . well, they're something to behold. But dawn is the real show.

Hipsters and poseurs shun Forest. That's why I like it.

When Laird died in 2012, Sara and I were between houses. We had sold our house in La Porte, Indiana, where we had lived for nearly twenty years, and were seeking to buy a new house near my new job in Mundelein, Illinois, a northern suburb of Chicago. Between selling the house in Indiana and buying one in Fox Lake, Illinois, Sara and I lived with my younger brother Mike in Elmhurst, Illinois, a western suburb of Chicago.

Monday through Friday we stayed at Mike's, but after school on Friday we drove down to Forest.

Sue died in 1999, so with Laird's death in 2012 the house in Forest had to be tended to, to be rid of accumulated stuff from Laird and Sue's fifty-year marriage and to be cleaned. The pole barn was the big question mark. Most of the stuff from the fifty-year marriage was in the pole barn.

Over the spring of 2012 Sara's sisters, their husbands, and all our children pitched in to spiff up the place. The property was not placed on the market until Sara and I purchased our new home in Illinois.

Those trips to Forest in the spring and summer of 2012 were great.

❖   ❖   ❖

Thursday, April 5, 2012: Holy Thursday

Second year in a row I've missed the Chrism Mass. It's such a beautiful Mass.

Tonight Sara and I are going to a church in Elmhurst for the Mass of the Lord's Supper. Tomorrow we head down to Forest, where we will spend Good Friday and Holy Saturday. Will go to Louann's for Easter Sunday dinner.

Monday, April 9, 2012:
Monday in the Octave of Easter

Isolated islands of puffy white clouds dot a deep blue sky. Wind and plenty of sun. Sunglasses on. Mild temp, but still I'm ensconced in my Wabash hooded sweatshirt complete with hood over my head, though the hood is up to thwart the strong sun from my nearly bald head, not to shield me against the cold.

Quiet. Only the wind sifting through the pines and maples make noise. Peaceful. Soothing to gaze out on the fields that will soon be planted with—with what? Corn? Beans? Who knows?

A hawk swoops down so low to the field that you would swear it was only a foot from the dirt. Looking for rodents, I suppose.

In the distance a car glides along County Road 600N. Can't hear the car; can only see it. Lonely. This place begs for prayer, it is so beautiful. If one can't pray here, one cannot pray at all.

Arrived here in Forest yesterday on the evening of Good Friday at about six o'clock. Sara and I attended the one-thirty Good Friday service at the cathedral in Lafayette, then ate at the Olive Garden. Called John before eating but didn't get an answer. Left a message. After we ate there was a message from John on my phone (which I had left in the car), so I called him back and asked if he wanted us to come and get him. A quick yes. All the other men in the house where he lived at Wabash College were leaving for the Easter weekend.

Saturday Sara's two sisters and their families arrived at Forest, and we cleaned up all the fallen limbs scattered about the property. The property looks the best it has looked in ages.

Saturday night Sara, John, and I attended the Easter Vigil at the cathedral in Lafayette. Two and a half hours. Loved it. The thirty-fifth anniversary of my being received into the Catholic Church.

Yesterday we drove over to Louann's for Easter dinner and to celebrate Laird's eighty-second birthday. He's at a nursing home in Fishers now. He'll never return to the house in Forest.

So now here I am. Praying and thinking and soaking in God. I'm within five feet of the field south of Laird's property, about seventy feet east of the barn. Corn was planted in this field last year. Now corn stalk stubble litters the field. Weeds struggle up through the dirt in the long furrows. Can *smell* the earth.

Have always presumed that reality rested where I worked and lived. *That* was real. But being here, seeing what I see, feeling what I feel, I now question that presumption. Here I don't project the false self. Here I relax and breathe and hear and feel God *more* than I do "back in the real world." Why can't this be real and that be false?

The city is false, pretentious, arrogant, and cold. Here God strolls and smiles and plays. Why would I want to leave that? The city is nothing more than modern Babel, humanity trying to conquer its angst with distractions of grandeur, noise, technology, and bluster.

Sara just called out the back door. Gotta go.

Later, 9:10 p.m.

So I'm back in Elmhurst. Airplanes roar overhead as they prepare either to land at or to blast off from O'Hare.

Back to work tomorrow, though no students (an in-service day). Worry about when we'll finally get a house. Classes to prep for. Anxious about being observed in class by administration (coming very soon for sure). In other words, more of the same gut-wrenching anxiety.

Need to get back to Forest.

Tuesday, April 10, 2012:
Tuesday in the Octave of Easter

Have already talked with Sara about heading back to Forest this weekend. She chose Forest. Will leave Elmhurst on Friday around 5:00 p.m., 6:00 Forest time (Eastern). That would get us to Forest about 11:00 that night. Stay until approximately 4:00 p.m. on Sunday.

Sara had a conference call with her sisters and the medical team at the nursing home where Laird is now living. Doctor said he'll never go back to Forest to live.

When he passes, the property will surely be sold. That's a shame. Yes, I'm the only one who loves the property, but the whole family has memories of it. Yes, I'd love to retire there, but Sara abhors the place. Can't ask her to live in a house she loathes. No realistic chance of ever really living here, so might as well sell it. I'd buy it if I could find a job in Kokomo, but I can't.

I remember years ago when we went to Sara's mother's family, the Hollises, somewhere out near Michigantown. I don't think Adam was born yet. The house where we met was out in the middle of nowhere, just as Laird's house in Forest is out in the middle of nowhere. I remember saying to myself how much I would love to live in such a place. The opportunity is so close to me now that I can taste it, but I can't close the deal.

Saturday, April 14, 2012:
Saturday in the Octave of Easter

Sara and I arrived back here in Forest last night about 10:00 local time. Rose early this morning and drove to the outskirts of Kokomo to fill a gas can at a BP station. Drove back here, poured some gas into the tanks of the riding mower, and mowed the entire place. Five minutes after I was finished, down came the rain.

Rain is forecast for the entire weekend.

Love it here. Absolutely love it. Prayer comes so easily here. Riding on the lawn mower praying memorized psalms!

Was indeed observed in yesterday's New Testament class. The principal arrived at my classroom right before the second bell rang. She stayed thirty-five minutes. Hope she liked what she saw. Need the job.

Has stopped raining for the moment (3:55), but more rain to come. Since it has stopped, I'm back outside. Love being outside here!

10:00 p.m.

Sara and I watched the evening fall while sitting on the porch. Sun was out for about ten minutes, but then the clouds returned and hid it. Still, a wonderful evening. Wish I could buy this house!

The Orthodox are bringing in Pasch this evening.

We're going to 6:30 Mass tomorrow morning for the Second Sunday of Easter. After that, breakfast and a visit to Laird. Want to squeeze in as much time here tomorrow as possible before heading back to Elmhurst.

Friday, April 17, 2012

Late (11:30 p.m.). Arrived here about an hour ago. Ate dinner at the Olive Garden in Lafayette.

Love being here. Laura and Louann are supposed to drive up tomorrow. Supposed to rain, too. Drat! Wanted to cut the grass.

Can't decide if I like coming here because I actually love it, or because Sara and I are alone. Probably both. I sincerely love it, see it almost as a hermitage. But I acknowledge that I enjoy the privacy we have here but lack at Mike's. That's not a criticism against Mike and Missy. They probably like it when Sara and I leave for the weekend. Then they can have some privacy!

Getting sleepy, so I'm going to bed. Night, all!

Wednesday, April 18, 2012

Last night about 11:15 the phone rang. It was Louann, calling to tell us that Laird had died.

His funeral is Sunday at 2:00 p.m. at a funeral home in Frankfort. Adam, Jenna, and John are coming. I'm picking up John from Wabash on Saturday at 9:00; Adam and Jenna are driving down to Forest on Saturday evening.

So both of Sara's parents are now gone.

I'm taking off work Monday.

Wednesday, April 25, 2012: St. Mark

The funeral this past Sunday went fine. I presided. All I did was Vigil for the Deceased and Rite of Committal directly from the rites book. The committal was short and sweet. Since Laird was a veteran, a color guard was present. The colors were handed to Adam.

About seventy-five people at the funeral, thirty for the committal. Laird was buried alongside Sue.

Sara's taking all this well, I think. Her greatest struggle is going back to the house in Forest. She loathes the house (too many bad memories and too far out in the middle of nowhere).

The Foxes invited us to brunch at their place not far from Forest. Laird's mother was a Fox.

So both of Sara's parents are dead. Of parents, only my dad remains.

Saturday, April 28, 2012

Rain. Prayed Terce outside on the porch a few minutes ago. Windy and raw. Feels good in the warmth of the house. While outside praying, I loved the sound of the rain falling, the wind in the pines, the sight of the farm fields across the road.

Beautiful.

Wednesday, May 2, 2012

One year ago today I had my job interview here at Carmel. Thank God for this job.

Already really looking forward to driving down to Forest this weekend.

Saturday, May 12, 2012

Early morning clouds have given way to blue sky and bright sun. Quiet. Just the birds singing and the wind in the trees. Just the way I like it.

So I look to you in the sanctuary to see your power and glory (Ps 62).

The sanctuary is this field of soy before me, the wind rustling the leaves of the trees, the coo of the doves, the vista of empty space, the quiet, the stillness, the peace of the prairie.

The sanctuary of the church is indeed holy, but so is this. Jesus is truly present in the Blessed Sacrament, but he is truly present here as well. Can't you feel him? His presence is palpable.

Curse the city! Curse its noise and bombast. A pickup truck barrels down County Road 600N, and the noise it makes comes and goes, drifting back into silence. Silence the norm.

But in the city noise is the norm, silence the anomaly. The elevated train is forever rumbling by. Planes overhead roar evermore. Cars honk, radios blare, jackhammers drill, people shout, trucks grind, and buses belch.

Streets in the city reek of cynicism. Talk-radio hosts compete with one another to be hip, sarcastic, and rude. All for laughs, of course. Billboards hawk these hucksters in a similar vein.

The mode of expression in the city is the wink and nod. The deal is cut beneath the table. Guile is prized, trust mocked.

Warns the psalmist,

> *For I can see nothing but violence*
> *and strife in the city . . .*
> *It is full of wickedness and evil;*
> *it is full of sin.*
> *Its streets are never free*
> *From tyranny and deceit.* (Ps 54:10-12)

Saturday, May 26, 2012: Vigil of Pentecost

Hot. The time/temperature sign in Russiaville (which I saw when I drove into Russiaville to pick up the pizza at Pizza King) said ninety-five. Ugh.

Arrived here in Forest at 11:30 and discovered that the electricity was off in the entire kitchen, including the refrigerator. All the beef, chicken, and pork in the freezer were spoiled, and oh my, did it stink! When we opened the door to the fridge, I gagged.

So I tripped the circuit breaker, and power immediately came back. How the power was tripped off is a mystery. No other section of the house lost power.

So now all my beer has to cool down!

No matter how well you think you know a community or monasticism by reading, it is only when actually living in a community that you actually know what the monastic life is about. So I can read all I want about monastic life, develop a fantastic monastic library, stay in the Monastic Center at New Melleray for a week once a year, but I will know nothing about the life, because I've never lived it.

Fourteen days, and I'll be at New Melleray.

8:15 p.m.

Sitting on the front porch. Sun dropping in the western sky. Robins flit about. More traffic than usual on County Road 600N. Still warm and muggy.

Across County Road 880E, which runs right in front of the house, corn grows in a huge field. I walked over there and stood in a row of corn; it reached the top of my socks.

Just love sitting here on the porch watching the corn grow! You know you're old when that's appealing!!

Trappist time tonight. Vigils at 3:30, then outside on the porch for Centering. Can't wait!

Sunday, May 27, 2012: Pentecost

A profound feast. Appropriate that the wind is forceful today. A good sign!

Sitting in the shade of a maple tree on the southern edge of the property. Before me, a field of soybeans. Except for the wind rushing through the trees, all is quiet. Hot and muggy— upper nineties.

The monks at New Melleray will pray Sext in fifteen minutes. And I sit here in the heat, humidity, and wind allowing God to wash over me. The quiet of the Pentecost Sabbath. How blest I am to be here.

The leaves of the soybeans waving in the wind. Far out into the field the waving transforms into applause.

The gift of prayer is beautiful, humbling, and precious. Prayer plugs you into the divine, allows you to feel God's presence, and opens your eyes to the sacred nestled deep within the profane.

Prayer is the domain of the faithful one. Religion without prayer is code. Prayer is more than the language of religion: it is the essence of religion. Without prayer religion dissolves into obligation, and a rote one at that. Prayer is to religion what water is to the crop.

Prayer is more precious than orthodoxy. The tribunal, the inquisitor, the prefect pale before the humble person of prayer. Thinking correctly is simple, and you can do so without prayer. Living in the image and likeness of God, however, is difficult, because it is impossible without prayer.

Words can be prayer. Jesus our Christ and Savior taught us to pray using words. But prayer can soar above words. In the throes of agony or in the rapture of joy, words to the Trinity can be superfluous.

Be still before the Lord (Ps 36:7); *Upon your beds ponder in silence* (Ps 4:5); *Be still and confess that I am God* (Ps 45:11). When Jesus spent the night in prayer (Luke 6:12), I'm guessing his verbal petitions to his Father were punctuated with periods of being still, of being quiet, of listening.

Prayer consumes the body, not just the soul. You and I are body *and* soul. The body is good. So standing, kneeling, walking, sitting, or prostrating—whatever feels right to you—do that. Put your body into prayer, not just your soul.

And finally this: don't dismiss pre-dawn prayer. Rise from your bed at 3:00 and step into the dead of night. Hear the silence, feel the peace, and consider the Lord and his strength.

What you taste while standing still in the night? That is a kiss from the Alpha and the Omega. And that's true whether or not you are in Forest, Indiana, or Chicago, Illinois.

Constantly seek his face. It's called prayer.

Friday, June 1, 2012

Last night at graduation, sitting on the floor of the Salvi gym at Carmel Catholic High School decked out in my academic garb, I was struck by this thought: forty years ago I was sitting on the floor of the gym at New Albany High School decked out in academic garb, waiting to receive my high school diploma. I could not imagine, *did not* imagine at that time forty years ago, that I would eventually be: (1) Catholic, (2) in north-suburban Chicago, (3) teaching theology, (4) a deacon, and (5) teaching at a Catholic school.

God has a sense of humor!

Graduation last night went well. Stuck around only briefly afterward. Congratulated several students and wished them well. On Wednesday night, before Baccalaureate, one of the mothers took a photo of her daughter and me together.

Overcast and cool. High today only in the low sixties. Rained all day yesterday and sprinkled some this morning.

Saturday Sara and I (and maybe John) will look at four houses. Will make a decision from there.

Wednesday, June 6, 2012

4:30 a.m.
The sixty-eighth anniversary of D-Day.
Four days until New Melleray.

Last night about 9:00 I received call from our realtor, Gina. She said that our offer for the house in Fox Lake had been accepted; we have a closing date of Monday, July 2.

Very excited about this!

No mortgage: we're cash.

Yesterday I completed my first academic year at Carmel Catholic High School. Faculty had to verify grades. I was walking out of the school by 10:15 in the morning.

Am very happy at Carmel.

So today begins my summer vacation. This is when the academic calendar pays off (well, Thanksgiving and Christmas, too)! But this summer will fly by.

9:00 a.m.

The corn across County Road 880E is now thigh high. A beautiful day here in Forest, Indiana, county Clinton. Deep blue sky, mild temp, and low humidity.

Received a nice e-mail from the father of Christian Raab, who is a monk down at Saint Meinrad. The father really liked my column about the Rule that appeared in the *Northwest Indiana Catholic* in June. Nice to know that my columns are being read by somebody!

11:25 a.m.

I seek God. Intellectually I know God is near, so near that God is actually carrying me. But emotionally . . .

Perhaps the better phrase is that I seek union with God. But even that phrase is lame. I have union with God in prayer and sacrament. I want to be completely enveloped by God. My sins keep that from happening, though.

Seems to me heaven is the endless, but joyful, absorption into God. The absorption will never end, because God never ends. An endless journey into the divine! The only thing analogous to that is sexual relations between husband and wife.

Island upon island of cotton-ball clouds float across the sky. Soft breeze, bright sun, mild temps, and the quiet of rural Hoosierdom. A glorious day!

Shadows race over the fields of corn and beans.

Sunday June 10, 2012: Corpus Christi

New Melleray Abbey
Rm. 305

Dawn. Birds quite noisy in the garth.

Arrived here yesterday about 11:00 a.m., so my first office of the retreat was Sext. As though I had never left. When I entered choir, Br. Felix was seated in the spot next to me, and he smiled that big smile of his and nodded. Great to be back in my monastic home! Love being here!!

After None Br. Paul Andrew met me in the cloister, and we chatted briefly.

June 2013 will probably be the next election for abbot. Fewer and fewer men carry the load of running the house. The others are just too sick or old. Stress of that load beginning to show.

Ava down to about four men who actually run that house. New Melleray's abbot is down there this weekend to try to work out a plan.

Holy Trinity in Utah on the verge of collapse. Average age is way up there. At best three men who carry the load of running the house, more like two.

The Monastic Center full, at least for today.

Worked yesterday with Placid planting corn. Neither of the other guys worked yesterday.

8:00 a.m.

After Lauds walked across Monastery Rd to Holy Family Church. Well, I didn't go in the church, but strolled the grounds around it praying the rosary. Still cool at the moment, but supposed to hit the low nineties today.

The view was beautiful looking out over the rolling field of corn. Prayed my usual prayer while gazing out over the maze.

When the house does elect a new abbot next year, changes—perhaps large ones—will certainly surface. The current abbot has been here for thirty years; by nature things will be different under a new abbot after so long being under one man. Couple that change with the dearth of new applicants, the aging of the community, and you have a recipe for potential problems.

Who will stand as abbot for election? I did not speak to Br. Paul Andrew about that.

Have the blinds closed here in my cell to keep out the morning sun and its heat. Actually, I slept well last night. Was comfortable in here.

Have *finally* purchased (from the gift shop downstairs) *RB 1980: The Rule of St. Benedict in Latin and English with Notes*. Have been wanting to buy it for years. So I bought it this morning. I'm going to purchase one more book, but I don't yet know which one. Will take my time on that one.

Since today is Corpus Christi, there is a procession after Mass.

Oh, and the abbot was back in his spot this morning at Vigils. Happy he's back! Speaking of Vigils, a nearly full moon this morning pouring through the windows. Wunderbar!

Back to the house being carried by fewer and fewer able-bodied men. In the late 1940s and early to mid-1950s, during the height of the monastic boom, the future acute drop of entrants could not be foreseen. Thus foundations were made to relieve the stress upon the existing houses. Quite understandable; the foundations were justified. However, some of those foundations are now foundering. Ava (foundation of New Melleray) and Holy Trinity (foundation of Gethsemani) are either at collapse or close to it.

However, from a strictly historical point of view this current situation is normal. The spike in entrants to monastic life after WWII was an anomaly. What we're experiencing now is more of the norm. Just as the houses after WWII had to adjust to the situation at that time (overcrowding), now the houses again have to adjust to their populations' reverting to their normal number. Just as it was painful after WWII (cost, uprooting monks from beloved houses, toil of building a new house), so it is painful now. As Jason Zuidema notes in his essay "More than Numbers: Monastic 'Presence' in Contemporary Canada,"

Anyone taking an even cursory glance at the consecrated life in recent Canadian, or even North American, history can see it is lived by those who are advancing in age and declining in number. By doing a little mathematical prediction, these same observers might come to the conclusion that it is only a matter of time, less than a generation even, until the religious life as it has been known in North America, more-or-less since the beginnings of European colonization, will be no more.[1]

However, God is in charge. God will provide!

Whoops, better be off to Mass.

10:30 a.m.

After Mass we processed. We exited the choir through the chapter room, processed through the cemetery, and then re-entered the monastery at the northeast end of the cloister, processed down the northern range of the cloister, and re-entered the church at the northwest end, processing back to our stalls.

Loved it. What I loved was its simplicity. No effort to embellish. No extravagant singing. No unnecessary liturgical garb or gadgets. Simply men processing in homage to the Lord with the abbot bringing up the rear with Our Lord in the Blessed Sacrament.

The chant we sang in procession was simple, with a very singable short refrain. The abbot *did not* employ the humeral veil. Thank God! Simply a man gifted with baptism holding in his hands the monstrance that bears Our Lord Jesus the Christ.

All efforts to make a more sacred atmosphere or to make the event more holy by heaping on humeral veils, cappa magna, myriad candles, armies of servers in cassock and surplice, bells, clappers, flower petals, and Latin hymns are vain. Such efforts are actually ludicrous, laughable really. How can human beings make better that which is already holy? Human beings cannot make something that is already holy more holy

[1] Jason Zuidema, "More than Numbers: Monastic 'Presence' in Contemporary Canada," *American Benedictine Review* 63, no. 2 (2012): 112.

by piling more stuff onto it. The proper thing to do is simply to allow the holy to speak for itself. That is exactly what was done this morning here at New Melleray in its Corpus Christi procession. Bravo!

That's the second time I've processed through the chapter room. The other time was at a funeral. How I love this place! How I love this life! Work a little, read a little, pray a lot!

Monday, June 11, 2012: St. Barnabas

New Melleray Abbey
Rm. 305
4:40 a.m.

Moments after Vigils began this morning rain began to fall. I was down in choir by 3:05, and by then lightning was dancing about. No thunder, but just as the subprior got us going with Vigils, down came the rain. The windows were open, and the cool fresh air rushed into the stuffy church. You could smell the rain, and it smelled sweet. You could almost taste it, actually. The rain did not come down in buckets. Rather, it was a steady firm rain. Now and then thunder grumbled in the distance.

The rain only accented the silence, and I don't think I've ever worshiped Vigils here so fervently. In the interval between the two nocturns the silence was so beautiful and sweet that resumption of the psalter was actually jarring.

At the conclusion of Vigils I remained seated in my stall just allowing the sound of the falling rain to wash over me. How blessed I was to experience God like that. My *lectio* this morning was appropriate: *Rejoice in the Lord always.*

And now the rain has diminished to a drizzle, the eastern sky hints of dawn, and the birds have begun to sing. Iowa is greeting the new day. God is walking among us.

11:10 a.m.

After Terce I walked over to the field of corn behind Holy Family Church across Monastery Rd. Simply beautiful. The wide expanse of rolling field, the corn waving in the wind, the quiet, the solitude. The low gray clouds blocked the sun, so the temp was comfortable. Humidity was up there, though. Tomorrow I'm going to walk to the crest of that same field. I'd say it's more than a quarter mile away, but less than a half mile (as measured from the back of the Holy Family church).

With each passing year the curtain that shrouds New Melleray, and by extension monasticism, lifts up another notch.

12:35 p.m.

Walking up the stairs to return to my room after the midday meal, and I see Fr. David Bock coming out of the gift shop. I say, "Hello, Father." He replies, "Hello Mark, how are you?"

How does he know my name?

Furthermore, yesterday the monk here who is the organist (along with Paul Andrew) stopped me yesterday afternoon as I was walking out on the front driveway. He was riding his bicycle. Said he, "You're Mark, aren't you?"

What's going on?

One of the men here in the Monastic Center lives near Gethsemani and is an Associate there. He knew Fr. Matthew Kelty well. Was a pall bearer at Kelty's funeral.

Haven't seen Fr. Stephen Verbest at all since I've been here. Hope he's ok.

Assume we'll be outside for afternoon work. Has not rained since early this morning.

7:00 p.m.

Very tired. Pitched hay this afternoon and cut spinach. Was very good work, though. Real Trappist work! Placid having me drive the truck all around the garden. "It is most important to realize that prayer is always God-given," Theophan the Recluse is reported to have said.[2]

---

[2] Igumen Chariton, *The Art of Prayer: An Orthodox Anthology* (New York: Farrar, Straus and Giroux, 1997), 98.

A new routine: before an office (but not necessarily *all* of them) I slowly walk down the full length of the northern and western ranges of the cloister. Very meditative.

Tuesday, June 12, 2012

New Melleray Abbey
Rm. 305
4:45 a.m.
The Lord is near.

The Lord is indeed near. Vigils this morning was sweet. When I awoke at 3:00, a half moon was spilling light into my cell. The air was calm and cool.

When I arrived in choir, Fr. Tom, of course, was already there. Quietly as possible I walked to my stall and sat down, conscious of not coughing or clearing my throat; it was just too quiet, too peaceful, too sublime to shatter the peace with such sounds. Outside . . . not a sound. No birds, no passing car along Monastery Rd., no plane or train.

Vigils is indeed *the* monastic hour. Whether or not one *always* feels what I felt this morning is really not the point. The point is that monks are privileged to have the opportunity to *experience* the sweetness of the Lord via Vigils. I'm happy I was able to do so this morning.

Now the eastern sky above the roofline of the monastery glows, the birds are singing, and life noises are beginning. Iowa is rising from its slumber. God has given us the gift of yet another day, and for me that gift is being at a monastery, *this* monastery. What will this day bring?

8:30 a.m.

The mere fact that a person is discerning diocesan priesthood tells me that he does not have a vocation to monasticism. A man who desires to enter a monastery desires *above all* to be a monk, *not* a priest. A man who is batting around the idea of being a priest is wasting his time batting around the idea of whether or not to enter a monastery.

At breakfast someone was talking about how peaceful this place is, how beautiful the life. He's right, of course. This place is peaceful; the life here is beautiful. However, he never once said to me that he desires union with God, that he seeks God. *That* is the reason a man enters a monastery.

Of course, he might not have said such a thing to me, because we hardly know one another; he might have thought telling me such thoughts—me nearly a stranger—too intimate to confess. What do I know, anyway? I'm a high school religion teacher who just *dabbles* in monasticism. I'm certainly no expert.

Yesterday, though, at one of our meals we got to talking about how politics is rampant in the Church. I told him that nothing, absolutely nothing, beats ecclesiastical intrigue. Then this morning, when he was listing the advantages of monasticism over secular priesthood, he mentioned that the monastery wouldn't have that.

Wrong. I would guess that politics is even more virulent here. First of all, people are people, whether they wear a business suit, Roman collar, or the cowl. Second, the very compactness of the monastery lends itself to cliques and alliances. Third, at *this* time at least, what with the election of a new abbot looming in the near future here at New Melleray, whispers I'm sure abound. Stances on positions are gingerly being sought. Monks are taking sides. In other words, politics.

Sunlight floods my cell. The bright cobalt-blue sky is clear; not a cloud to be found. The humidity is low. Just a hint of a breeze. The air smells sweet and clean. All is quiet, save the occasional passing of a car or truck on Monastery Rd. God dances about. Can't you see Him? Feel Him? I am so blessed to be here.

Time for Terce.

10:50 a.m.

Just returned from walking over in the cornfield across the road. Walked all the way to the crest of the field praying psalms. Beautiful. I sat cross-legged in the field, in one of those wide swaths of field not planted with any kind of crop, just a path—so to speak—for farm equipment to travel to and fro within the field.

God was dancing about in that field. The sky so blue, the air so cool and fresh and clean and dry. The bright sun felt good. Crows cawing and robins singing. One of the most beautiful sights I have ever seen. I thanked God for allowing me to see what I saw, hear what I heard, feel what I felt, and taste what I tasted. The real presence of God there was as strong as any time before the Blessed Sacrament.

Came out of the church after Terce stepping into the cloister at the northwest end, and the abbot was standing there. We said hello. I heard the abbot introduce himself to the guy walking behind me, and they both retired to the abbot's office. I headed for the field across the way.

Upon coming back up into the Monastic Center after my walk in the field across the street, I heard a couple of people talking, a monk and one of the other guests. I went to my room, but then headed back to the kitchen here in the Monastic Center, and as I was about to step into the kitchen, both of them stepped into the hallway. From *The Art of Prayer*:

> First of all it must be understood that it is the duty of all Christians—especially of those whose calling dedicates them to the spiritual life—to strive always and in every way to be united with God, their creator, lover, benefactor, and their supreme good, by whom and for whom they were created. This is because the center and the final purpose of the soul, which God created, must be God Himself alone, and nothing else—God from whom the soul has received its life and its nature, and for whom it must eternally live. For all visible things on earth which are lovable and desirable—riches, glory, wife, children, in a word everything of this world that is beautiful, sweet, and attractive—belong not to the soul but only to the body, and being temporary, will pass away as quickly as a shadow. But the soul, being eternal by its nature, can attain eternal rest only in the eternal God: He is its highest good, more perfect than all beauty, sweetness,

and loveliness, and He is its natural home, whence it came and whither it must return.[3]

Amen to that!
Let's go pray Sext, shall we?

1:05 p.m.
Walked around the parking lot and prayed the Joyful Mysteries of the rosary (prayed the Sorrowful ones earlier this morning).
Placid will have us in the garden for sure this afternoon.

Wednesday, June 13, 2012: St. Anthony of Padua

New Melleray Abbey
Rm. 305
5:05 a.m.
The anniversary of my first starting to pray the Liturgy of the Hours. I believe it's the sixteenth anniversary, but I'm not sure. At any rate, a blessing from God for which I am eternally grateful.
Another cool morning. I slept with the windows open last night, but I also placed a wool blanket on my bed.
Birds talking up a storm out in the garth.
Spoke with Hal Jopp yesterday evening. Was good speaking with him, for we hadn't conversed in a while. Turns out he's going to be at Saint Meinrad in August, at the same time I'm leaving my retreat at Gethsemani. So I'm going to swing by Saint Meinrad after my stay at Gethsemani to see Hal. Also, we're going to meet here at the Monastic Center next June for retreat. I don't think I've seen Hal for at least three years.

8:25 a.m.
A new person has arrived here in the Monastic Center. Have yet to see him; he was not at Vigils, Lauds, or Mass this morning.

---

[3] Chariton, *Art of Prayer*, 46–47.

When I spoke with Sara last night on the phone she asked me to pull up Jenna's blog, as I did after talking with her. Very nice entry by Jenna about John staying at their place this summer.

Also, Sara had spoken with Gina, our realtor, who said she is working to close on our house *before* the official close date of July 2. Would be nice!

When it comes to the monastery, there is always an area of the house forbidden to me; there's always an activity I cannot participate in; there are always persons with whom I cannot speak or have difficulty speaking with. At Gethsemani there is the hated sign, "Do Not Enter: Monastics Only." Here, I'm not welcome in the East or South range of the cloister. Of course, all the living area is off limits, as well as the library. Last night at 7:15 the bell rang, and the monks gathered in the chapter room. Felix and Xavier were in choir praying when the bell rang. One of the postulants was in the choir as well when the bell rang. Felix and Xavier got up and walked into the chapter room, and Xavier said as he passed the postulant, "Let's go to chapter." The postulant followed Xavier into the chapter room.

Intellectually, I know that makes sense. If Sara, Adam, Jenna, John, and I meet as a family, only the family is welcome to attend. Only family is welcome to certain sections of my house. Similarly, I am not a member of the family of New Melleray; I'm more like a friend of the family. It only makes sense that I am not welcome in some places of the house.

Still cool. Sky not as brilliant as yesterday; clouds are forming.

Time for Terce.

10:00 a.m.

Sitting on the lawn directly behind Holy Family Church. I'm near the edge of the vast rolling field of corn. One of my favorite vistas here at New Melleray.

Exiting the cloister after Terce, both of the other people from the Monastic Center are stopped by Fr. David and Fr. Jonah respectively.

Thursday, June 14, 2012

New Melleray Abbey
Rm. 305
2:45 a.m.

We play in our minds a certain film, titled "My Life." The plot of this film is our life, the way we see it playing out in time. We see our life unfold—or we see how we think we would like to see it unfold—and we concoct all kinds of scenarios on how that will happen and what it will look like.

We are the heroes of this film, of course. Not only that: we're its writers and directors. Thus the film always plays out the way we want it to play out.

Believing that the film is real is dangerous. What is real is not that film in our minds, but the events that transpire in our daily lives outside of our heads. And though we can plan and schedule our life, ultimately stone-cold reality makes itself known in ways that often cut us to the quick, that have nothing to do with that film in our heads. Disappointment and humiliation are the fruits of believing in the film.

8:40 a.m.

Simplicity and authenticity: always seek them. Is what I am doing true, authentic? Or is it forced, pretend, and unreal? Is what I am doing simple? Or is it artificially elaborated in order to impress?

One of the men who has been here with me left right after breakfast. Joining us late in our breakfast was one of the monks. Said that the abbot is "very eager" to relinquish being abbot. Eight months until he retires. I asked him about the spirit of the house. He said it's good, but there is also a high level of anxiety.

He also said that Ava is near collapse. A Vietnamese monk has been brought in as superior.

10:20 a.m.

Do I truly seek God?

I've come as far as I am able in the Monastic Center. I can wear this smock the entire time I'm here, pull up the hood, and disappear into it. But doing so means nothing. Hence my aversion to wearing it outside of choir. I wear it only in choir or when I'm in my cell (and even then only rarely). All other times—including at meals—it's off. To wear it otherwise, in my opinion, is an empty gesture.

The Monastic Center here at New Melleray has been a wonderful gift, and I will continue to delight in the gift. But I am acutely aware that *monasticism* is being lived across the garth, not here in room 305.

Do I truly seek God? Yes, but distractions avert my attention.

1:00 p.m.

Received a call from Fr. Heeg. He and some other priests are on retreat at Mundelein, and he called to see if we could get together for supper. Obviously, a no go. But we sure had a fine conversation on the phone. He sounded good.

My last full day. Has been great, wonderful actually. Leave tomorrow after Terce. Drive straight to Adam's place in Chicago. Sara and I will spend the night at Mike's. Saturday morning at 8:00 we have the home inspection for the place at Fox Lake. From there Sara and I head down to Forest, where we'll stay for a week. We'll come back to Mike's for the week of June 25. We close on the house Monday, July 2; the movers bring our furniture that's been in storage since March on Tuesday.

The next time I come to New Melleray it'll be from my Illinois home.

Will clean my room here in the Monastic Center after Vigils tomorrow morning. I still should have some time for deep prayer before Lauds at 6:30. Since only Kevin and I are here in the Monastic Center, my making noise cleaning my room after Vigils shouldn't present a problem.

7:00 p.m.

Tired. Placid worked us to 4:30. I enjoy it, though. I'm pleased that he allows me to drive his truck around.

Should sleep well tonight.

Saturday, June 16, 2012

This Bloomsday evening finds me in good ol' Forest, Indiana. Yes because I like the place don't you know and I ate my breakfast at the table with a couple of eggs yes!

Thunder grumbles in the distance. Rain pitter patters, but we need a good soaking. The cornfield across 880E is ash dry.

Sara and I prayed the Eleventh Sunday in Ordinary Time at St. Mary Cathedral in Lafayette this evening.

The men at New Melleray are in choir singing Compline right now.

The rain smells good. The rain *sounds* good; it sharpens the silence.

With our upcoming move to Fox Lake I'm going to have to weed my library. Loath to do it, but must. There is simply no space for a lot of my books.

Sunday, June 17, 2012:
Eleventh Sunday in Ordinary Time

Arrived back in Chicago from New Melleray in the early afternoon on Friday. Yesterday morning, Saturday, was the home inspection of the property in Fox Lake. All went well. Close on Monday, July 2.

Arrived here in the early evening yesterday, after having attended the Vigil Mass at the cathedral in Lafayette.

The plan is for us to stay here in Forest all week. Yeah! Since we do not have internet access here, I'm driving into Frankfort tomorrow to see if I can have access there (e-mail, pay bills).

Lazy Sunday afternoon. Sitting on the porch here in Forest reading the long introduction in *RB 1980* and reading psalms in my ongoing psalter (up to Psalm 56). Finished a cycle of the psalter while at New Melleray. Would like to finish this one before the end of June.

Later:

A warm night, a cold beer, *RB 1980* and a setting sun in a quiet field of corn. Doesn't get any better than that.

Monday, June 18, 2012

Forest, IN

Blistering hot. Ninety-seven today.

Early this morning, at 7:30, I was atop the roof of the house trimming the hedges that had risen above the gutter line around the front and south side of the house. Then I trimmed all the hedges, raked up the trimmings that had fallen, and, using the lawn mower with the little trailer hooked up to it, carried the trimmings back to the burn pile.

Real Trappist work! Placid would have been proud, I hope!

Was finished by 11:30. Exhausted. Stopped around 9:00 to pray Terce.

After eating lunch, Sara and I drove to the Frankfort Public Library to check e-mail.

Tuesday, June 19, 2012: St. Romauld

Brutally hot day here in Forest. Now, at 8:45 p.m., it's still in the upper eighties.

Sitting on the patio I cleared off this morning. Quiet.

I can very well understand why Laird both loved this place and was loath to leave it. It's peaceful here in Forest. One can think, dream, and feel a connection to the earth.

Thursday, June 21, 2012

Forest, IN

Rain, finally! Need it so badly.

Sitting out on the porch this morning at 3:30. Stars so clear and bright you think you could reach out and touch them. Very quiet, though two cars did drive by, one on County Road 880E!

Take John back to Chicago tomorrow (we picked him up yesterday from Adam's), but we're right back here tomorrow evening. Will be here through Tuesday. Head back Wednesday.

Close on house at Fox Lake a week from this coming Monday.

Received e-mail from my nephew Travis.

Hope it rains all night.

Friday, June 22, 2012

Pigeons coo. A cardinal sings. A car swishes by on County Road 600N. You hear it in the distance, and as it draws closer, the sound grows louder. It swishes by, and the sound dies. Only the birds and the bugs.

Living here has shown me this: I want to live in the country.

"Silence is most friendly to divine love."

Adam of Perseigne[4]

I will attest to that! Have to Google Adam of Perseigne. Here is a usual day in Forest:

---

[4] Adam of Perseigne, Letter 9, in *The Letters of Adam of Perseigne*, trans. Grace Perigo, CF 21 (Kalamazoo, MI: Cistercian Publications, 1976), 103.

I rise about 4:15 a.m. I step out onto the porch and pray Vigils. After Vigils I walk in the yard, soaking in the silence. I eventually grab a lawn chair and plunk it down to the south side of the house in order to watch the dawn.

Go back in the house for *lectio*. Later, when the sun is strong, I return outside to pray Lauds. Since the grass is wet I pray Lauds pacing up and down 800E.

After Lauds, pray the rosary, again while pacing up and down 800E right in front of the house.

Next up is breakfast: cereal, OJ, toast, and fruit. Now it's 7:00 or so, and I begin my work outside. I start early to beat the heat. Depending on what needs to be done, I continue work till 9:00, at which time I pray Terce.

Return to work, but finish by 11:00. I shower and spend the remainder of the day reading, writing, and praying the Office. The quiet and solitude is not only conducive to this sort of schedule: it is also precious.

This, it seems to me, is the way to live.

I'm going to look back at this spring and early summer of 2012 and smile. Staying here at Forest has been a blessing—a gift—and I will look back on this time here with fondness and pleasure.

Sunday, June 24, 2012: Birth of St. John the Baptist

Sara and I prayed Mass this morning over at the cathedral in Lafayette.

Yet another hot day. The rain we received last week wasn't enough, only about a half inch.

Week from tomorrow we close on the house in Fox Lake.

Pounded out my August column for the *Northwest Indiana Catholic*. Will transmit to Debbie tomorrow.

Tuesday, July 3, 2012

Installed!

This past Thursday we closed on the house in Fox Lake, and today the movers brought our furniture from storage in Michigan City, Indiana, where it's been since early March. Glad we hired movers, for the temp is brutal: one hundred.

The movers were supposed to be here between 9:30 and 10:00. They arrived at 11:00. "We made a wrong turn," said one of the two movers. Neither of them could have been older than twenty-two.

Sara and I are exhausted.

However, tomorrow is the nation's 236th birthday. Let's crank up Sousa!

❖   ❖   ❖

Listen to Merton:

> Man has an instinctive need for harmony and peace, for tranquility, order, and meaning. None of these seem to be the most salient characteristics of modern society. Life in a monastery, where the traditions and rites of a more contemplative age are still alive and still practiced, cannot help but remind men that there once existed a more leisurely and more spiritual way of life—and that this was the way of their ancestors. . . .
>
> We would like to be quiet, but our restlessness will not allow it. Hence we believe that for us there can be no peace except in a life filled up with movement and activity, with speech, news, communication, recreation, distraction. We seek the meaning of our life in activity for its own sake, activity without objective, efficacy without fruit, scientism, the cult of unlimited power, the service of the machine as an end in itself. And in all these a certain dynamism is imagined. The life of frantic activity is invested with the noblest of qualities, as if it were the whole end and happiness of man.[5]

[5] Thomas Merton, "The Contemplative Life in the Modern World," in *Thomas Merton: Selected Essays*, ed. Patrick F. O'Connell (Maryknoll, NY: Orbis Books, 2013), 226.

Forest, Indiana, is where I experienced "peace, tranquility, order, and meaning." Not that I had not experienced such things before; I had. Rather, I experienced those things *not* in a monastery. The goal, the end, so clear at New Melleray, Gethsemani, or Saint Meinrad, was just as keenly experienced in Forest. I don't think I had understood that before.

However, lest you think that "peace, tranquility, order, and meaning" can be found only—or usually—in quiet out-of-the-way places, consider the following two stories. Both true.

True story number one: years ago when Sara and I were first married and lived in Indianapolis, we drove a hundred miles south to my hometown of New Albany, Indiana, to visit family.

One evening as dinner draws near, my grandmother—my mother's mother—offers to buy us all a pizza. Now, my grandmother is on a tight budget, and so she isn't able to splurge. However, she insists that she, and she alone, buy the pizza. Thus, she offers to buy one large pizza . . . for seven adults, including my two younger teenage brothers.

My mother quickly becomes agitated at my grandmother's offer. Mom knows that purchasing enough pizza for all of us is not in my grandmother's budget. So my mother offers to purchase two large pizzas as well as an additional small one.

No deal. My grandmother wants to be the sole purchaser of the meal. My mother and grandmother haggle over this for a good ten minutes. Finally, they strike a deal: my grandmother will buy one *extra-large* pizza.

My grandmother beams.

However, the pizzeria where we're going to buy the pizza? It does not even offer extra-large pizzas. Mom knows this. It's a sop to my grandmother.

Someone places the order, and another ventures off to fetch the pizza.

Minutes later here it comes. The pie is placed on the kitchen table and the box is opened. Everyone looks at the one large pizza and then at one another. No way is it enough.

Then my mother makes her move. Grabbing the pizza cutter she proceeds to slice the pie into very narrow slices. She places two miniscule slices on everyone's plate and announces—dead serious, I kid you not: "See . . . everyone gets two pieces."

Now, let's suppose my mother had prevailed. Let's suppose my grandmother had relented in letting my mother buy enough pizzas to actually feed everyone. The episode would have been forgotten after eating the pizzas. We wouldn't have a story that my family likes to tell over and over again.

And the story is what matters. For the story is a living illustration of Jesus' command, *Love one another* (John 15:17).

You see, my grandmother just had to show her love for us. At the time this took place she was quite old. She believed herself to be a burden on my mother, who cared for her. Sara and I lived two hours away, and we rarely saw my grandmother anymore. Here was a chance for her to show how much she loved us while everyone was gathered together. She would feed us.

Mom knew it wasn't enough pizza, but she also knew how much it meant to her mother to be the sole purchaser of the pizza. So she relented. And my wife, my brothers, and I played along, knowing it would make my grandmother happy.

But that outpouring of my grandmother's love could be seen only in hindsight. At the time it was complete consternation for my mother and total amusement to the rest of us. But that is what my grandmother did, that was her goal: to serve her family.

Jesus us tells us to love one another. How that love is carried out may—at the time—appear to be something other than love. And you don't need to live in a monastery to figure that out.

Codicil to the story: later that evening Sara and I went to a restaurant to eat. We were hungry. While we were there, my dad walked in to get something to eat.

True story number two: when Sara and her sister Louann were children and living on Palmer Street in Frankfort, Indiana, Laird and Sue—Sara and Louann's parents—often had

Aunt Betty Hollis, Sue's sister, babysit for them while they went out by themselves for the evening. In an effort to thwart Aunt Betty's scheme to walk the kids downtown for a snack, Laird and Sue would dress Sara and Louann in their pajamas when they dropped the two girls off at Aunt Betty's house. Pajamas meant bedtime!

Aunt Betty would have none of it. She simply draped a light coat over the girls, and the three marched down to the Dog 'n' Suds, about a quarter mile from the house. Now, Dog 'n' Suds is your classic drive-in; you know, the car pulls up to a slot where there is a menu and speaker. You place your order via the speaker, and the server, who was always a girl at the time this story took place—late 1950s—places the tray on which your order rests on the slightly rolled-up window of your car.

Since Aunt Betty never owned a car—she never in her life possessed a driver's license—the three marched up to a side window of Dog 'n' Suds and placed their order there: three root beer floats. When the order was delivered, they sat at a nearby picnic table reserved for walk-ups. Root beer floats always taste best at such places.

Aunt Betty never married. She lived her whole life in that one house on West Barner Street in Frankfort. She supported herself for most of her life by working at Murphy's Five & Dime (long gone) down on the town square. She walked to work. She had six brothers and six sisters. (Despite the fecundity of her parents, the family was not Catholic. That sometimes surprised people. That says more about them than about the Hollis family.) Growing up, the whole crew lived in that house together on Barner. One bathroom. Several to a bed. The old man, a Republican, rode the rails for the Nickel Plate Railroad. The mother, an FDR Democrat, cooked and cared for her brood. The old man liked to smoke cigars. He also liked his girly calendars. The mother banished the scantily clad nymphs to the cellar (where the coal bin used to be), with the understanding that at Thanksgiving and Christmas said nymphs had to be removed. Fine.

When you came to visit Aunt Betty she always welcomed you as if she hadn't seen you in fifty years. She doted over you and made sure you had a Coke and something good to eat, like a slice of pie or a peach or a ham sandwich lathered with mayo. At Christmas, the whole crew gathered in the house at Barner (adults upstairs and kids in the cellar, where there was an old washtub filled with ice and Cokes). The paper plates were all set out at the tables for the big dinner. Plastic forks and spoons sat atop paper napkins. Beneath one of the many napkins placed at the kids' table? A dollar bill. When it was time to eat, all the kids rushed to a seat and quickly slapped over the napkin. "A body needs spending money no matter how old they are," said Aunt Betty.

By the time I got around to visiting Aunt Betty when Sara and I first started dating, Aunt Betty was old. Around the house she wore that apron all the time as well as black, old-lady shoes; you know, the ones like your fifth-grade teacher wore. She laughed easily, and her blue eyes were soft, but alive. She always seemed happy. When you left from your visit with her, she seemed genuinely disappointed you were leaving. She always invited you back.

Aunt Betty's nieces and nephews adored her. Even people who were in no way related to her called her Aunt Betty. That's who she was; she was everyone's designated Aunt Betty.

Her funeral was a simple affair. Her remaining siblings who could make it and those nephews and nieces who could attend stood in a circle around her coffin in the mausoleum, recited the Lord's Prayer, and then in unison cried out joyfully, "My Aunt Betty!"

Don't you see? Her family was her purpose, her goal.

"To throw yourself before God, not to measure your progress, to leave behind all self-will; these are the instruments for the work of the soul," said Abba Poemen.[6]

---

[6] *The Sayings of the Desert Fathers: The Alphabetical Collection*, ed. Benedicta Ward, CS 59 (Kalamazoo, MI: Cistercian Publications, 1975), 172.

Those instruments can be played by monk or citizen. Yet it is in the monastery, it seems, that those instruments seem to be tuned and played most often. That's why people flock to the monasteries: they want to play the instruments too.

"Are you hastening toward your heavenly home?" asks Benedict.[7] We are, or are at least trying to. Some of us, fewer and fewer at this point in time, seek the heavenly home via monasticism. More and more of us, hastening toward our heavenly home, seek at least to take a first step into the cloister. But that's as far as we want to go, or can go. So be it. Let God sort it all out.

Jean Leclercq was optimistic about it, I think: "Aspirants will appear if God wills it as he has willed it for centuries. Nothing in contemporary civilization leads us to believe that those who are called will refuse."[8]

Perhaps different kinds of aspirants are being called? Different from those in the past?

"Are you hastening toward your heavenly home?" On this side of existence, at least, it's all about the journey! Don't look back. Keep moving forward. Nothing is behind you. You only think there is something back there. Push ahead. Awake the dawn, not the dusk.

Matthew Kelty noted,

> As the world needs poets, priests, dancers, dreamers, artists, singers, prophets—all of them devotees of sign and symbol—so too [it needs] monks who live in touch with reality. This in turn becomes both model and inspiration for all caught in the materiality of the material, out of touch with the hidden glory that is all around us.[9]

[7] RB 73.8 in *RB 1980*, ed. Timothy Fry (Collegeville, MN: Liturgical Press, 1981), 207.

[8] Jean Leclercq, *Aspects of Monasticism*, CS 7 (Kalamazoo, MI: Cistercian Publications, 1978), 173–74.

[9] Matthew Kelty, *My Song Is of Mercy* (Kansas City, MO: Sheed & Ward, 1994), 214.

I've said it once, and I'll say it again: monasticism is about reality. That's why it intrigues people so. I used to think that there was such a thing as lay monasticism. I no longer believe that. Rather, I believe there is monasticism, and the fullness of that life lies with the monks, followed by oblates, with the rest of us wannabes and hangers-on straggling behind. One big group.

Of course, in fifteen years (if I'm still on this side of the sod) I may change my mind. Nothing wrong with that. Shows I haven't given up thinking about it.

Never underestimate photographs. Terryl N. Kinder's *Cistercian Europe: Architecture of Contemplation* and David Heald and Terryl N. Kinder's *Architecture of Silence: Cistercian Abbeys of France* sit on my bookshelf at home. Now and then I take them down and leaf through the pages, admiring the pictures. I would like to see those monasteries in person someday, not just in photographs. I would especially like to see Fontenay and walk the cloister there. I would also like to see Maria Laach in Germany and Einsiedeln in Switzerland.

Do you think monks ever take down such books and look at them, or are such books only for those of us who don't live in monasteries? The only evidence I know about this is from Merton:

> Later in the afternoon Dom Frederic placed in my hands one of the most beautiful books I have ever seen. It is an album of pictures of one of our ancient Abbeys, in Provence— Senanque is its name. Both the photographs and layout are wonderful. I was very happy.[10]

Looking at picture books of monasteries doesn't necessarily make me happy, but looking at the photographs does seem to calm my spirits.

[10] Thomas Merton, *Entering the Silence: Becoming a Monk and Writer*, ed. Jonathan Montaldo, *The Journals of Thomas Merton*, vol. 2, 1941–1952 (New York: HarperSanFrancisco, 1997), 37.

There is danger, though, in spending too much time with such books. Oh, I don't mean danger to your soul or anything drastic as that. Rather, the danger I'm thinking of is its distorting reality. You look at the photographs, and you begin to imagine things. And all of a sudden Gregorian chant—like the recorded stuff that sounds so good—starts playing in your head. My point: picture books like that, though nice, tend to project an unreal image of monasticism as lived today.

Monks don't live at Fontenay, folks.

A phone. Have you noticed that people don't use the word *telephone* anymore? No one says, "Hey, can I use your telephone?" It's "Give me your phone."

A phone. It's a misnomer. True, it is a telephone, but not nearly as much as a device to tweet, snapshot, take pictures, or play games. Yet we call it a phone.

It reminds me of the "mumps" episode in Mark Twain's *The Adventures of Huckleberry Finn*. Huckleberry runs into Susan and makes up this crazy story about Mary Jane taking care of Hanner, who supposedly has the mumps. Huckleberry tells Susan that Mary Jane has been sitting up all night with Hanner. All a lie, of course.

"Mumps your granny!" Susan tells Huckleberry, smelling something wrong. "They don't set up with people that's got the mumps."

Huckleberry then tells Susan that people sure do sit up with people who have *these* mumps. He tells her that *these* mumps are a new kind, because they are mixed up with other things, such as whooping cough, erysipelas, yellow jaundice, and brain fever.

"My land!" Susan says, "And they call it the MUMPS?"

Huckleberry responds, "Because it IS the mumps. That's what it starts with."

Then Twain writes the punch line through the voice of Susan: "Well, ther' ain't no sense in it. A body might stump his toe, and take poison, and fall down the well, and break his neck, and bust his brains out, and somebody come along and ask what killed him, and some numskull up and say, 'Why, he stumped his TOE.' " [11]

Perhaps the current state of monasticism is like Twain's mumps or the current phone. It's got all this other stuff mixed in at this point in history—monks, oblates, lay associates, fans, wannabees, old and odd—and only time will sort it all out. In the meantime we're all credulous, as is Susan, while stumping our toes trying to make sense of it all.

Well, that's all I got. I know it's not much, but bulk was never my forte. Those towns in Illinois, Indiana, and Kentucky seem long ago. Forest seems like forever ago. Speaking of Forest, Laird's property was indeed sold. The guy who owns the property next door put up a cow shelter and placed it so close to the property line that it made Laird's old property less desirable. Sara and I have driven by it exactly twice since the place was sold (en route to visit her sisters near Indianapolis). The new owners have added a chicken coop. I'm counting on seeing Placid and Paul and the subprior next June. Hope to see Hal there too. I'll see Ptacek tomorrow. His classroom is just across the hall, and you can take it to the bank that monastic life will pop up somewhere in our conversations, either before or after school or between classes. I'm urging the director of music at my parish to attend Columba Kelly's workshop on chant next summer. I know he would love it.

Mom? Memory of her is growing dimmer as the years pass. Sara and I will be celebrating our fortieth wedding anniversary in three months. We'll probably do a bourbon tour and stay at the Beaumont Inn in Harrodsburg, Kentucky. This will be in December or early January. Like hell I want to share Kentucky with the Big Heat and his good friend Mr. Humidity in the middle of July. Don't want to even think about walking through a rackhouse in summer. I think Sara's sister and her husband

---

[11] Mark Twain, *The Adventures of Huckleberry Finn* (New York: Washington Square Press, 1970), 245–46.

are coming along, too, so that will be nice. Dad will probably meet us there for dinner one evening along with his wife Dee.

But in the long run? I'm going to buy me a Ford Super Duty F-250 XLT 6.2 liter gasoline V8 pickup truck and head for the North Woods. Or as Huckleberry says, "I reckon I got to light out for the territory." You know, cool summers and bone-chilling dark winters with piles of snow. That's my kind of territory. If only Mom could hear me say that; she would shake her head and make a fist with her right hand and say, "Oh, Mark!"

But that is what Mom never understood: there is no end to the search.

Coda

"It's too romantic!"

So what?

How is a love affair *supposed* to start out? Jaded? Cynical?

I was seventeen years old when I first met Sara. I was knocked out. She was wearing a short green skirt, and her breasts teased beneath a cream-colored blouse. Her thick blond hair fell over her shoulders and tumbled to her derrière. She was standing on four-inch heels, and her green eyes sliced right through me.

The thunderbolt, man.

As I said, Sara and I will be married forty years. *Stability*. We have two grown sons, two daughters-in-law, and two grandchildren. I'm sixty-two years old as I write this. Is my love for Sara the same now as it was when I was seventeen? No way. My love for her is stronger now. Deeper.

But I needed to be struck by the thunderbolt before I could reach the level of love I have for her now. I needed that romantic blastoff.

So do those who enter monasteries.

If a romantic disposition is the first step to a golden anniversary of matrimony, just so a romantic view of the monastery is the first step toward a jubilee within the cloister.

The central question is: What do you seek?

Somewhere, sometime, and in a manner that cannot be explained, a woman or a man is struck by the thunderbolt of the monastery. Have you been struck by that thunderbolt? Fear not its jolt.

Amice ad quid venisti?

Appendix A:
New Melleray Antiphonary

TUESDAY – TERCE

℣. O God, ✠ come...

HYMN

PSALMS 119, 120, 121

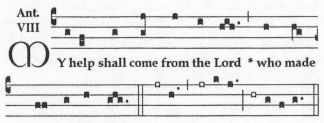

Ant.
VIII

Y help shall come from the Lord * who made

heav-en and earth.

The rest as at Terce, (ORD 9).

TUESDAY – SEXT

℣. O God, ✠ come...

HYMN

PSALMS 128, 129, 130

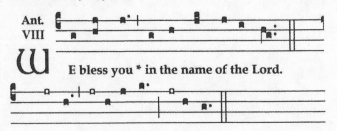

Ant.
VIII

E bless you * in the name of the Lord.

The rest as at Terce, (ORD 9).

OFFICE ORDO   June   Week I

26 Sun <u>THIRTEENTH SUNDAY IN ORDINARY TIME</u>
         TEM 27   Vig: 1010
                                               Lds: 1031
                                               Vps: 1217

                                               BEN: 1158
                                                    1197
                   Compline Hymn #2
              Second Nocturn Recited this Week

27 Mon Mem of Saint Cyril of Alexandria   Lds: 1055
        BpDoct   Vps: 1117
        Zech COM 32 Mary COM 33

28 Tue Mem of Saint Irenaeus BpM   Lds: 1059
        Zech COM 27   Vps: 1161
        1st Vespers of Peter and Paul SAN 159

29 Wed <u>SAINTS PETER AND PAUL</u> App   Vig: 1164
        Solemnity SAN 161   Lds: 1162
                                             Vps: 1161

30 Thu Mem of the First Martyrs of Rome   Lds: 1055
                                             Vps: 1117
                        July

1 Fri Mem of Saint Junipero Serra Pr   Lds: 1059
                                             Vps: 1092

2 Sat Mem of Our Lady   Lds: 1193
        Zech COM 13   Vps: 1345
        1st Vespers of 14th Sunday TEM 29

Appendix B:
Graduale Triplex

SANCTUS XVIII

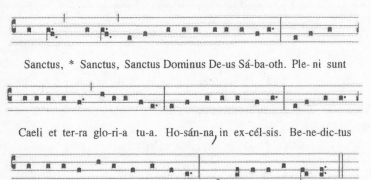

Sanctus, * Sanctus, Sanctus Dominus De-us Sá-ba-oth. Ple- ni sunt

Caeli et ter-ra glo-ri-a tu-a. Ho-sán-na in ex-cél-sis. Be-ne-dic-tus

Qui ve-nit in no- mi- ne Do- mi- ne. Ho- sán na in ex- cél- sis.

An English language setting

Ho- ly, * ho- ly, ho- ly Lord, God of hosts.

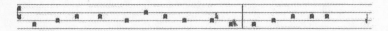

Hea-ven and earth are full of your glo- ry. Ho- san- na in the

high- est. Bless-ed is he who comes in the name of the Lord.

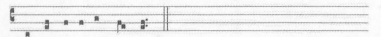

Ho- san- na in the high- est.

THE ORIGINAL NOTATION

Communion antiphon *Comedite pinguia*, in E 121

THE NOTATION IN THE GRADUALE TRIPLEX

Communion antiphon *Comedite*, in Graduale Triplex, p.268

Appendix C:
Daily Schedule for the Three Monasteries

New Melleray

3:15	Rise
3:30	Vigils
4:00	Scripture / Private Prayer / Breakfast
6:30	Lauds
7:00	Mass
8:00	Scripture / Private Prayer
9:15	Terce
9:30	Work
11:45	Sext
12:00	Dinner
12:30	Scripture / Private Prayer / Rest
1:45	None
2:00	Work
4:30	Scripture / Private Prayer / Supper
5:30	Vespers
6:00	Scripture / Private Prayer
7:30	Compline
8:00	Retire

Sunday Mass is at 9:00.

Abbey of Gethsemani—Weekday		*Gethsemani—Sunday*	
3:00	Rise	3:00	Rise
3:15	Vigils	3:15	Vigils
5:45	Lauds	6:45	Lauds
6:15	Eucharist	10:20	Terce
7:30	Terce	10:30	Eucharist
12:15	Sext	12:15	Sext
2:15	None	2:15	None
5:30	Vespers	5:30	Vespers
7:30	Compline	7:30	Compline

Saint Meinrad Archabbey—Weekdays		*Saint Meinrad—Sunday*	
5:30	Vigils & Lauds	7:15	Vigils & Lauds
7:30	Mass	9:30	Mass
12:00	Noon Prayer	12:00	Noon Prayer
5:00	Vespers	5:00	Vespers
7:00	Compline	7:00	Compline

Bibliography

Adam of Perseigne. *The Letters of Adam of Perseigne.* Translated by Grace Perigo. CF 21. Kalamazoo, MI: Cistercian Publications, 1976.

Beales, Derek. *Prosperity and Plunder: European Catholic Monasteries in the Age of Revolution, 1650–1815.* Cambridge: Cambridge University Press, 2003.

Bernard of Clairvaux. *On the Song of Songs II.* Translated by Kilian Walsh. CF 7. Kalamazoo, MI: Cistercian Publications, 1983.

———. *Sermons for the Autumn Season.* Translated by Irene Edmonds. CF 54. Collegeville, MN: Cistercian Publications, 2016.

Casey, Michael. *The Art of Winning Souls: Pastoral Care of Novices.* MW 35. Collegeville, MN: Cistercian Publications, 2012.

———. "Monasticism: Present and Future; Part II." *American Benedictine Review* 65, no. 3 (2014): 296–311.

———. *Toward God: The Ancient Wisdom of Western Prayer.* Liguori, MO: Liguori/Triumph, 1996.

Cassian, John. *Conferences.* Translated by Colm Luibheid. Classics of Western Spirituality. New York: Paulist Press, 1985.

Chariton, Igumen. *The Art of Prayer: An Orthodox Anthology.* New York: Farrar, Straus and Giroux, 1997.

The Cloud of Unknowing and The Book of Privy Counseling. Translated by William Johnston. New York: Doubleday, 1973.

Cummings, Charles. *Monastic Practices.* MW 75. Rev. ed. Collegeville, MN: Cistercian Publications, 2015.

Eckerstorfer, Bernhard A. "The Challenge of Postmodernity to Monasticism." In *Church, Society and Monasticism: Acts of the*

International Symposium, Rome, May 31–June 3, 2006, edited by Eduardo López-Tello García and Benedetta Selene Zorsi, 111–24. Rome: Pontificio Ateneo S. Anselmo, 2009.

Evagrius Ponticus. *The Praktikos[;] Chapters on Prayer.* Translated by John Eudes Bamberger. CS 4. Kalamazoo, MI: Cistercian Publications, 1981.

Gregory of Nyssa. "Oratio 6." In *De beatitudinibus*. PG 44:1194–1303.

Heschel, Abraham Joshua. *The Insecurity of Freedom.* Philadelphia: Jewish Publication Society of America, 1966.

Kardong, Terrence. *Benedict's Rule: A Translation and Commentary.* Collegeville, MN: Liturgical Press, 1996.

———. "Thoughts on the Future of Western Monasticism." In *A Monastic Vision for the 21st Century: Where Do We Go from Here?* edited by Patrick Hart, 57–72. MW 8. Kalamazoo, MI: Cistercian Publications, 2006.

Kelty, Matthew. *My Song Is of Mercy.* Kansas City, MO: Sheed & Ward, 1994.

Kinder, Terryl N. *Cistercian Europe: Architecture of Contemplation.* Grand Rapids, MI: Eerdmans, 2002.

Kinder, Terryl N., and David Heald. *Architecture of Silence: Cistercian Abbeys of France.* New York: Harry N. Abrams, 2000.

Leclercq, Jean. *Aspects of Monasticism.* Translated by Mary Dodd. CS 7. Kalamazoo, MI: Cistercian Publications, 1978.

———. *The Love of Learning and the Desire for God.* Translated by Catherine Misrahi. 2nd ed. New York: Fordham University Press, 2007.

The Liturgy of the Hours. New York: Catholic Book Publishing Company, 1975.

Louf, André. *The Cistercian Way.* CS 76. Kalamazoo, MI: Cistercian Publications, 1983.

Mencken, H. L. *The Vintage Mencken.* New York: Vintage Books, 1955.

Merton, Thomas. "Blessed William of Saint-Thierry: Monk of Signy." *Cistercian Studies Quarterly* 35, no. 1 (2000): 5–12.

———. *Entering the Silence: Becoming a Monk and Writer.* Edited by Jonathan Montaldo. *The Journals of Thomas Merton.* New York: HarperSanFrancisco, 1997.

———. *Selected Essays.* Edited by Patrick F. O'Connell. Maryknoll, NY: Orbis Books, 2013.

———. *The Waters of Siloe.* New York: Harcourt Brace, 1949.

Pennington, M. Basil. "The Benedictine Contribution to Evangelization." *American Benedictine Review* 49, no. 2 (1998): 222–29.

RB 1980: The Rule of Saint Benedict. Edited by Timothy Fry. Collegeville, MN: Liturgical Press, 1981.

Sommerfeldt, John R. *Bernard of Clairvaux: On the Spirituality of Relationship.* New York: Paulist Press, 2004.

Studzinski, Raymond. *Reading to Live: The Evolving Practice of Lectio Divina.* CS 231. Collegeville, MN: Cistercian Publications, 2009.

Twain, Mark. *The Adventures of Huckleberry Finn.* New York: Washington Square Press, 1970.

Ward, Benedicta. *The Sayings of the Desert Fathers: The Alphabetical Collection.* CS 59. Kalamazoo, MI: Cistercian Publications, 1975.

William of St. Thierry. *Exposition on the Song of Songs.* Translated by Columba Hart. CF 6. Kalamazoo, MI: Cistercian Publications, 1968.

———. *The Golden Epistle.* Translated by Theodore Berkeley. CF 12. Kalamazoo, MI: Cistercian Publications, 1971.

Zuidema, Jason. "More Than Numbers: Monastic 'Presence' in Contemporary Canada." *American Benedictine Review* 63, no. 2 (2012): 112–21.